BECOMING A NEW PERSON
Twelve Steps to Christian Growth

Philip St. Romain

LIGUORI
PUBLICATIONS

One Liguori Drive
Liguori, Missouri 63057
(314) 464-2500

Imprimi Potest:
John F. Dowd, C.SS.R.
Provincial, St. Louis Province
Redemptorist Fathers

Imprimatur:
+ Edward J. O'Donnell
Vicar General, Archdiocese of St. Louis

ISBN 0-89243-200-4
Library of Congress Catalog Card Number: 83-82855

Cover design by Pam Hummelsheim

Table of Contents

Introduction

During the past fifty years, millions of people throughout the world have broken free from obsessive-compulsive behaviors by practicing a set of principles that lead to Christian growth, serenity, and joy. Alcoholics, drug addicts, overeaters, and gamblers are among the many different kinds of self-help groups utilizing a Twelve-Step approach to personal and interpersonal renewal. Not since Ignatius of Loyola developed his program for the spiritual development of his Jesuits in the sixteenth century has such a comprehensive and systematic approach to Christian growth been embraced by so many.

Twelve-Step programs have been more successful in arresting obsessive-compulsive behaviors than any other rehabilitative approach offered to date. Their principles are practical, comprehensible, and seemingly applicable to all. They presuppose no level of intellectual sophistication other than the ability to communicate verbally and, perhaps, a minimal literacy. In addition, they emphasize spiritual renewal without embracing any particular religious denomination and/or set of dogmas. Thus do they bring the healing power of God to many who, for various reasons, have not been able to find such graces within their religious tradition of choice.

Who originated the program?

The formulation of the Twelve-Step program to rehabilitation can be credited to a New York stockbroker and an Akron, Ohio, physician, Bill W. and Dr. Bob, respectively, both cherished as co-founders of Alcoholics Anonymous. They, in turn, often readily acknowledged their indebtedness to the alcoholics with whom they worked as well as a variety of professionals, including philosopher William James, psychiatrist Carl Jung, an Episcopal priest named Sam Shoemaker, and a physician named William D. Silkworth. But the deeper origins of modern self-help programs can be traced to Oxford Groups, a Christian renewal movement popular earlier in this century.

Not to be confused with the Oxford Movement, which was the brainchild of John Henry Newman and other Anglican clergy who followed in his footsteps, Oxford Groups began as a result of the ministry of Frank Buchman. A Lutheran minister who had experienced somewhat of a falling-out with his governing committee in America, Buchman journeyed to England, where he was blessed with a vision of a Christ-led, sin-free world. He began working tirelessly to bring about the realization of this vision, finally converting two Cambridge undergraduates and inviting them to assist him in the evangelization of Oxford University. Their success was phenomenal, Oxford becoming a Mecca of sorts for thousands of lay people as well as professional ministers, who all sought a whiff of the spiritual breezes blowing around the exalted center of learning. During the 1920s and 1930s, the movement spread throughout the world, gaining tens of thousands of enthusiasts. A non-denominational venture, Oxford Groups helped many people return to their respective traditions with a better understanding of what is true and essential in Christianity. Its goal — nothing less than a Christian spiritual renewal of the whole world — seemed almost to be within grasp for a while; but, through the war years, the movement began to die away. It is practically impossible to find an active Oxford Group today.

An alcoholic friend of Bill W., named Ebby T., found sobriety through his Oxford Group involvement in August 1934. Ebby T. gave witness of this to Bill W. who, on the verge of death and despair from his own alcoholism, was both encouraged and frustrated with the implications of his story. Somewhat an agnostic, Bill W. could not easily open himself up to the possibility of being healed by God from a malady that was, for all practical purposes, considered untreatable. In December 1934, Bill W. was hospitalized for acute alcoholism. When he heard that Dr. Carl Jung had declared alcoholism incurable except for some kind of spiritual experience, he was distressed; he felt he was incapable of such an experience. But after his attending physician, Dr. William D. Silkworth, counseled him concerning his impending doom, he pleaded for God's touch from the depth of his being. His prayer was answered — one of those earthshaking, twice-born religious experiences that turns lives upside down. He never drank again.

During the months that followed, Bill W. and Ebby T. worked closely with Oxford Groups in an attempt to help other alcoholics find sobriety. In this venture they were miserable failures, scaring off as many drunks with their confident spiritual enthusiasm as they did Oxford Groupers, who embraced a wider ministry. Growing discouraged, Bill W. journeyed to Akron, Ohio, in May 1935, on a business venture that was to prove financially disastrous. He became tempted almost beyond sanity to get drunk, but decided to call a minister and ask for a list of alcoholics with whom he might speak. Thus hoping to lose himself in a healthy venture, he was led to Dr. Bob, a hopeless addict nearing the terminal stages of his own illness. Bill decided to tone down his religious enthusiasm and discuss instead the futility of trying to self-will oneself out of addiction. While traveling to Dr. Bob's home, he recalled William James' writings concerning the necessity of ego-deflation as a prerequisite to the twice-born experience, inspiring him to try a different approach in witnessing. He discussed with Dr. Bob his own past illness, prompting the physician to take what in effect came to be called his first Step: admission of his powerlessness over alcohol and the unmanageability of his life. The two went on to become co-founders of Alcoholics Anonymous, whose membership now exceeds 1,000,000 in over 80,000 groups meeting worldwide.

Bill W. and Dr. Bob worked closely with Oxford Groups from 1935-1937, when they finally broke away to embrace a narrower scope of ministry to alcoholics only. The Twelve-Step approach to rehabilitation from alcoholism they developed represents a systematization of Oxford Group principles, especially as articulated by Father Sam Shoemaker. The informality of the typical AA meeting was modeled on Oxford Group House Party gatherings, where prayer, study, testimonials, and exuberant fellowship predominated. Oxford Groupers' insistence on the social equality of its members inspired, in part, the AA tradition of anonymity (which was also emphasized because of the moral stigma attached to alcoholism). Unlike Oxford Groups, however, they posited a healing Higher Power not necessarily grounded in the person of Jesus Christ. They also de-emphasized pressure tactics and other practices that tended to raise the already rigid ego defenses of their alcoholic members. Through their work, the legacy of Frank Buchman lives on.

Do "healthy" people need this help?

It is a paradox that this — one of the most spiritually potent movements in history — should be reserved now for the most broken and impotent people in the world. Somehow this seems in keeping with the spirit of Jesus Christ, however. Many who are "healthy" can appreciate the help that people are getting through Twelve-Step programs and can recognize the validity of the renewal Steps. (Most religious traditions emphasize a version of these principles to some degree.) But healthy people hesitate at taking Step 1, which must be taken if the other eleven are to be successfully completed. If one is not an alcoholic or an overeater or a gambler, why take Step 1, which invites an acknowledgment of the destructiveness of a personal vice? What if one is not obsessively, compulsively addicted to any particular vice?

Not too long ago — before the "death of God" movements undermined our notions of a God of judgment — most people were imbued with a sense of sin. Ministers leaned heavily on a forensic notion of humanity as criminal before a just God, who demanded repentance and acceptance of his Son as a way back to grace and eternal life. How to turn the minds of "healthy," "guiltless" people toward God has been the ministerial challenge of the 1970s and 1980s. Enter the Gospel to the Guiltless.

The Gospel to the Guiltless has presented Jesus as the one who came not so much to save us from sin as to show us the way to become fully human. The prominence of Jesus' role as Redeemer was de-emphasized, making way for a reverencing of his role as Revealer. Truth replaced sacrifice as the way to spiritual growth; for sin came to be identified more as ignorance than as rebellion. In Twelve-Step language, Steps 1 and 12 were lopped off, leaving a beautiful set of principles but little potency. In its most perverted form, the Gospel to the Guiltless became the Gospel of Self-Fulfillment, sanctioned by a God who sent his Son "that they might have life and have it to the full" (John 10:10). It is a Gospel minus the Cross.

To say that genuine spiritual renewal is happening today only in Twelve-Step groups would be narrow-minded arrogance, of course. Still, it may be argued that wherever lasting renewal is happening these Twelve Steps are being practiced in some manner. Among religious groups of "healthy" people, our addiction to selfishness can be recognized as our stumbling block to growth. Steps 2-11, never very controversial in the first place, might be seen as positive suggestions for moving away from selfishness toward relationship with God and other people. Step 12 becomes our outreach, challenging us to go beyond the convenient circle of family and friends to extend the Good News of grace to the whole world.

How to use this book

The pages which follow include discussions of and suggestions for utilizing the Twelve Steps of self-help programs as guides to spiritual growth. For Step 1, I have substituted the word *selfishness* for the words *alcohol, food,* etc., calling attention to the insidious ways in which selfishness robs us of growth. For all those Steps involving a relationship with a Higher Power, I have developed a Christian notion of what this might mean. Twelve-Step programs presuppose a God who is at least pro-health and pro-growth, both of which are qualities of the Divine, drawing heavily on Judeo-Christian revelation for their support. I am, therefore, hopeful that these Twelve Steps to growth might now be more deeply embraced by those already practicing them in some manner as well as by those who have avoided them because of the stigmas attached to Step 1.

Most Twelve-Step programs encourage Step completion under the direction of a mature group member designated as a sponsor. But there are many variations of moving through the program. In certain treatment settings, for example, Step completion is carefully supervised by counselors, who provide excellent guidebooks for assistance. Outside of formal treatment settings, many members proceed at their own pace, moving along when they feel they are ready. Group meetings occasionally include special teachings concerning the practicing of a Step, for one is never really through working this program.

Because nothing like a Twelve-Step Christians Anonymous program exists today, the individual using this book will have to find his or her own communal context for support in living out these principles. If at all possible, one's first journey through the program ought to be taken in dialogue with another mature Christian. Perhaps this book could be used as the basis for forming a Christian support group; if you cannot locate such a group, then start one yourself. But if you choose to move through the program without the benefit of a spiritual director or a support group, you should at least begin considering who will help you to work through Step 5. Whether working alone or with others, move along at your own pace, completing the Steps in the sequence listed in this book. As long as you are making progress, there is no need for you to rush yourself.

This program works! It has proven itself to be a tool of the Spirit on innumerable occasions. It is not a trendy experiment in Christian spirituality, being grounded instead in the most basic truths of Christian tradition. All that remains is for you to tap the graces that will come to you if you are faithful in practicing these principles.

(Note: Some of the chapters in this book contain a follow-up *Personal Reflection* and a *Group Discussion*. But where the contents of the chapter already embody a personal reflection, only a group discussion is presented.)

1

We admit that we cannot realize our fullest human potential by living a life of selfishness

Christian theology and human experience teach us that the main reason why we do not experience lasting joy on earth is because selfishness often perverts our noblest strivings and motivations. Sin can be described as a force that separates people from God and, hence, from one another. This is what selfishness does to us.

In contrast, a healthy self-love enables us to strike a balance between overestimating and underestimating our talents. Self-love requires a truthful acceptance of ourselves in all our strengths and limitations, and this is the wellspring of love for others. Selfishness deprives us of self-love, however, blinding us to truth and acceptance by keeping us in a state of unhealthy desiring.

Sin came into the world when our first parents decided to use their free will in such a manner as to express an unrelated and rebellious independence. If we are honest, we can identify these same tendencies in ourselves today. "I cannot even understand my own actions," we often say with Saint Paul. "I do not do what I want to do but what I hate," he laments in his Letter to the Romans (7:15). We shall have to strive against these insidious energies within us until we die.

If we allow ourselves to live completely according to the dictates of our lower, selfish nature, we shall become creatures with less dignity than lower animals, who are at least true to their own natures. But human beings are far more than instinctual animals. There is a self in us that longs for beauty, truth, love, justice, and wisdom; and we possess a capacity for consciously realizing these values in our lives. If we do not experience these spiritual qualities in any degree of intensity, it is probably because we are living more on the side of our selfish nature. Saint Paul writes: "It is obvious what proceeds from the flesh: lewd conduct, impurity, licentiousness, idolatry, sorcery, hostilities, bickering, jealousy, outbursts of rage, selfish rivalries, dissensions, factions, envy, drunkenness, orgies, and the like" (Galatians 5:19-21). Few would consider this to be a portrait of the joy-filled life.

Because selfishness is so manifestly bad for us in the long run, why do so many of us nonetheless fall into its snares? The main reason has to be that there are payoffs in pleasure, esteem, and security — three of the strongest reinforcing emotional states. If selfish behavior could consistently deliver pleasure, esteem, and security, we might not be able to offer an effective critique of the selfish life. The truth is that these feelings are generally short-lived, requiring an ongoing diet of self-indulgence for their sustenance. In the case of pleasure, sensual gratification for selfish ends leads to a diminishment of pleasure in the long run; similarly, that which gives a sense of esteem and security can usually be taken away, undercutting peace of mind and spiritual growth. Shortsightedness is responsible for a great deal of our selfish behavior, but breaking free is not easy.

Most people recognize the folly of living a completely self-indulgent life. Through the centuries, many have proposed moral laws and other codes of conduct to help minimize the clashing of selfish wills in society. Although such laws have been very helpful in generating harmony among people, they still leave the human spirit starved for something more. Staying out of trouble is better than getting into trouble, but it is not enough.

We hunger for so much, yet seem capable of realizing so little. "There is nothing better for man than to eat and drink and provide himself with good things by his labors" (Ecclesiastes 2:24). "Life is suffering," Buddha proclaimed as the first of his Four Noble Truths; and he added that selfish desiring is at the root of our suffering. "Most people lead lives of quiet desperation," said Thoreau hundreds of years later. Selfishness kills the human spirit, but dare we hope for more from life?

Jesus and the rich young man

In Saint Mark's Gospel (10:17-22), we read the story of a rich young man who had been a faithful Jew all of his life. He had probably heard Jesus teaching on a few occasions and had become impressed by the peaceful joy and strength that emanated from him. One day when Jesus was on a journey, this young man broke through the ranks of disciples and other followers surrounding Jesus and knelt at his feet. "Good Teacher, what must I do to share in everlasting life?" he asked in earnest, oblivious to the scornful reproach on the faces of Jesus' disciples. Jesus gave him his full attention, however, for he recognized real urgency in the young man's voice. "No one is good but God alone," he said. "You know the commandments," he added, listing a few honored by people in all cultures. The young man looked up at Jesus somewhat disappointed. "Teacher, I have kept all these since my childhood," he replied. Jesus placed a hand on the young man's head and gazed at him in love, for here was a true son of Abraham.

"There is one thing more you must do," he challenged. "Go and sell what you have and give to the poor. . . . After that, come and follow me." At this the young man scrambled to his feet and began to back away. Jesus continued to hold out a hand to him, but the young man's expression had hardened.

Why did this young man seek out Jesus in the first place? He had youth, wealth, and a clear conscience. Opportunities for pleasure, power, comfort, and security opened out before him in ways that most people would have envied. Yet, it was not enough for him, and it is to his credit that he recognized his entrapment and sought a way out of his material and psychological suffocation. As the cynical philosopher, Schopenhauer, put it, "life vacillates between suffering and boredom." Most likely our rich young man was bored. "Is this all there is?" he probably asked himself time and again. Not until he saw Jesus did he hope for a way out of his quiet despair, but when Jesus invited him to become a disciple he balked. Letting go of his attachments was inconceivable to him.

From this episode in the life of Jesus we learn that legalistic observance of the commandments does not bring deep joy. We also see that Jesus has come not only for those who are broken in health and spirit but also for the many who are comfortable and empty. Like the rich young man, however, we must be willing to be honest enough with ourselves to examine our lives to see if we are satisfied or if we yearn for more. Like him, too, we must be willing to bring our yearnings before Jesus. Unlike him, we must respond in obedience to Jesus' invitation to accept God's gifts of grace in our lives.

Human longings

Several questions naturally emerge at this point. Why was our rich young man not entirely content in his situation? How is it that so many people with abundant opportunities to achieve esteem, pleasure, and security so seldom find deep and lasting joy? These are questions that bite at the heart of human nature, provoking the most pointed inquiry of all: What is it that human beings really need?

Through the years there have been many responses to these questions. Various philosophers and psychologists have identified the following to be high on the list of human longings: the esteem of others, sexual fulfillment, assurance of immortality, money and the things money can buy, material security, love and belonging, knowledge, harmony, and self-actualization. Few would deny the relative importance of each of these motivators, but none seems capable of providing an all-encompassing focus worthy of the totality of human nature.

Philosophers speak of human behavior as springing from one of three levels of our nature. They distinguish between body, mind, and spirit. First, we are *physical creatures,* and sensual gratification is an important and essential motivating factor. After all, without food or drink we would eventually die; and without the use of sex our species would become extinct. The payoff for sensual gratification is pleasure, which reinforces the gratifying behavior. Second, we are *psychological beings,* capable of using our minds to understand ourselves and our world. Our memory, reason, feeling, and imagination can be placed at the disposal of consciousness to help us make decisions and attain knowledge, love, self-respect, and the esteem of others. When we experience these values we feel well-being, happiness, and security. But there is a third level. We are also *spiritual beings,* hungering for beauty, freedom, and wisdom — in short, meaning. In our quest for experiences of meaning we utilize our minds and our bodies, but it is in our spiritual faculties that these needs are embraced. When we do perceive ourselves to be meaningful, the consequent peace, joy, and inner confidence illuminate our minds and our bodies.

We were designed to live on a spiritual level, but selfishness keeps us confined to lower levels. People who live for sensual gratification — good food, drink, sex, etc. — identify these sources of pleasure as their meaning in life. They ignore the psychological and the spiritual. Similarly, people who make knowledge or power the supreme values in life corrupt their spiritual faculties in the process. Healthy spiritual persons are those whose hunger for meaning embraces truth and love, norming their sense of meaning with humility and community. What is insidious about sin is that we shall automatically regress to a lower level of character if we do not constantly strive to realize meaning in truth and love. If we're not progressing, we're regressing. This is a basic rule in the spiritual life.

The rich young man was a good, intelligent person. He probably had considerable control over his bodily passions, for he was moral and living on at least a psychological level of motivation. He felt empty inside, however, and that is the problem with many of us. We might manage to stay out of trouble, but life still seems dull and meaningless. But if we would leave this world of the living dead, we'd best be prepared to do the kind of thing Jesus asked the rich young man to do: let go of our sources of false security, whatever they may be. We shall not have to struggle on our own power though. The good news is that there is grace aplenty for all who want to become growing, joyful, spiritual human beings.

Change of heart

Those who want to accept Jesus as leader must learn to deny themselves, take up their crosses, and follow in the steps of Jesus (see Mark 8:34). If we want to grow into the fullness of our human potential in Christ, we shall have to turn away from those behaviors and modes of thinking that have kept us selfish. This will mean a change of heart. But in order to turn away from these destructive practices, we must first identify them and see them for what they are. Here are some examples of common self-indulgent behaviors and modes of thinking:

1. *Anger:* Although it is possible to be angry for a just cause, most of our anger comes from unfulfilled expectations. Upon close and honest examination, these expectations usually turn out to be self-centered. It is safe to assume that, unless we are engaged in a prophetic venture, anger is probably a sign of selfish thinking.

2. *Sexual irresponsibility:* This refers to sex outside the context of a committed relationship. Even if the other party consents to this kind of an arrangement, our capacity for developing deep and meaningful relationships with members of the opposite sex is weakened. Such recreational sex is usually fueled by the fires of self-indulgence and, so, must be purged from our thinking as well as behaving.

3. *Gluttony:* Overindulgence in food and/or mood-altering chemicals is a sign that we are living more on a physical than spiritual level — although in some people this has become an illness over which they have no control. Nonetheless, Alcoholics Anonymous and Overeaters Anonymous emphasize spiritual renewal as a way back to health and sanity.

4. *Jealousy:* By lusting after the possessions of another, we erect a wall between ourselves and them. Also, materialism spawns many of our envious desires, and materialism is usually a form of greed.

5. *Greed:* Whether or not we legitimately earn wealth is not the issue in condemning greed. Greed means wanting more than

we need and refusing to share with others. This only worsens our unrelated desiring, causing us misery.

6. *Ambition:* It is one thing to strive to better ourselves, but quite another to be compulsively driven to do so — especially at the expense of others. Ambition becomes a pitfall when it moves us to be manipulative and oppressive as we pursue our goals.

7. *Laziness:* This is the opposite of ambition, but is equally destructive to the human spirit because it allows our talents to stagnate from disuse. By refusing to develop and utilize our potential, we deny ourselves the energy and respect that come from engaging in the movement of life. The consequent apathy and inertia are counter-spiritual.

8. *Self-righteousness:* An overvaluing of our opinions and self-regard lead to an inflexible righteousness. This is one of the most insidious forms of selfishness because it robs us of openness to changing other destructive behaviors. Jesus had some of his greatest difficulties with self-righteous people.

9. *Self-pity:* Occasions for legitimate grief and anger can lead to self-pity if we allow them to rob us of a renewed effort to engage ourselves in life. Self-pity is usually based on a sense of deservingness that is proud and narrow-minded. At any rate, it is always counter-productive.

Any of the above or combinations thereof cause mental fragmentation and factions among people. They retard our thought process and divide us from ourselves and from one another. Unless we learn to move away from these kinds of practices toward more healthy and meaningful behaviors and thought patterns, we shall never achieve the kind of internal unity that is a prerequisite for building unity among people.

At this stage in our renewal, our main concern should be that we recognize selfish behavior as leading only to very short-term pleasure and long-term pain. In the Steps that follow, we shall undertake a process for growing out of selfishness into spiritual fullness. But unless we are absolutely convinced that the life we want to save is destroying us and our world, we will not be able to properly appreciate God's way to life revealed in Jesus Christ.

Personal Reflection

In order to identify the ways in which selfishness disrupts your own spiritual growth, you will need to spend some time examining your behavior and motivations. Many people have found that writing a journal is a helpful means to reflect upon life. You might also consider using questions such as those which follow to help you get in touch with your own selfishness.

1. What occasions most often provoke you to anger? What expectations of yours are violated at that time? How do you generally express your anger? How does this affect others?
2. Do you encourage sexually irresponsible fantasies in your mind? How does this affect your relationships with people of the opposite sex?
3. Do you maintain a proper diet with regard to food and drink? How do your eating and/or drinking habits affect your health? Your relationships with others?
4. How do you treat the people with whom you work on a professional level? Have you ever manipulated others in order to advance yourself and your interests? If so, does it now seem to have been worthwhile in terms of spiritual growth?

5. Is procrastination a problem for you? Have you allowed relationships once important to you to lapse because of laziness? What kinds of tasks necessary for your spiritual growth have you put off lately?
6. What do you most envy in other people? How does this affect your relationships with them? Would you really be better off if you obtained the object of your envy?
7. If you have been guilty of self-pity, think back on what occasioned it. Have you worked through these feelings? How does self-pity affect your relationship with others?
8. Which opinions of yours do you find it hardest to change? Are you open to constructive criticism from others? Why? (Why not?) Are you open to ongoing conversion, or do you feel as though you have "arrived" at spiritual growth?
9. Draw a symbol or picture that represents to you what living a life of selfishness does to you. Place this illustration where you will see it regularly to remind you of the kind of life you are rejecting.

Group Discussion

1. What is the difference between selfishness and self-love?
2. How does selfishness frustrate the desire for pleasure, esteem, and security? Share some examples from your own life.
3. Share some of your responses to the personal reflection questions above. (Share only those you feel free to discuss.)
4. How do laws help people to live together more peacefully? How adequate are laws in curbing human selfishness?

2

We confess that Jesus Christ can lead us to the fullness of life

It used to be fashionable to ask people if they believed in God. Many supposed that the Theory of Evolution disproved God's role as Creator of the world, while others reckoned that psychology could give us all we needed for self-understanding and motivation. During the past thirty years, theologians and scientists have grown considerably in their understanding of the mutual dependence of their disciplines; only philosophical regressives still cling to the preconceptions of the nineteenth century and its rationalism. With recent polls indicating that over ninety percent of Americans believe in at least a Creator-God, perhaps it is appropriate to ask here: ''Who is your God?''

When it comes to the question of God, there are, in the last analysis, only three possible conceptions; but within each of these there is considerable variation.

1. *Polytheism* (from *poly* meaning several and *theos* meaning god) is belief in several more-or-less equal claimants of one's devotion and life service. These gods might be conceived of as spiritual beings vying for power in the universe (as in the ancient Greek religions.) Practically speaking, they may be as mundane as job, country, family, and even

church if a person sets any of these up as primary objects of "worship." Because polytheists pursue several of these ends, they may become mentally fragmented as they struggle to make sense of a universe that pulls them one way and then another.

2. *Dualism* is belief in two counter, or complementary, principles. The Yin-Yang of Chinese cosmology and the good-evil of Zoroastrianism and certain tangential Christian philosophies are cases in point. Real progress toward good is not hoped for since there is no reason to believe that good can last very long. These systems of thought breed fatalism and ethical stagnation — sometimes more so than certain polytheistic philosophies.

3. *Monotheism* is belief in one God or Power whose influence in creation is at least indirectly decisive. Monotheistic systems include some Eastern religions, Platonism, and several other philosophies, and the Judeo-Christian-Islam tradition. God's attributes vary widely among these belief systems, but all foster a unification of mind and personality and help focus the will toward a primary set of life issues. Certain ideals such as family, country, or career are primary motivating ideals in the lives of many, but it might be stretching the point a bit to consider them secular forms of monotheism.

With so many belief systems abounding through cultural history, one is tempted to draw back in confusion and give up the struggle to know God at all. History shows quite clearly that religious beliefs have spawned some of the most dehumanizing waves of malice, prejudice, and warfare ever evidenced on planet Earth. Why indeed bother with the question of God?

The answer to this question lies in the irrefutable fact that something within us yearns to understand the meaning of creation, life, work, birth, suffering, and death. Our minds see the movement of life as a relationship between cause and effect, and so we naturally ask, "From whence comes the ultimate cause of the effects we see about us?" Nihilists — those who believe that all traditional values and beliefs are unfounded — have been unable to answer this question by positing for us a world of blind chance with no beginnings, ends, or meanings.

We all reach a point sometime when we must ask the two essentially religious questions: "If there is a God, then what is God like?" and "What does God expect of human beings?" Keeping these questions in mind, we may now turn our attention to Christian beliefs concerning Jesus of Nazareth.

Jesus of Nazareth

Everything we know about Jesus of Nazareth comes to us from within the context of Christian faith traditions. The few secular references to him say very little, and most seem to draw their information from the Church anyway. It would, therefore, be impossible to speak about Jesus without utilizing biblical information concerning his life, ministry, and meaning. Apart from the New Testament, we know very little about Jesus.

Because the New Testament is so obviously an expression of the faith of the early Church, many have raised questions concerning the literal historicity of its contents. During the past century, Scripture scholarship has made much headway in this area; we now realize that the authors of the Gospels were not trying to write historical documents in accord with the norms and constraints of twentieth-century historians. They give very little information that might be useful to historians, being concerned instead with the meaning of Jesus' life and ministry, death and Resurrection.

There are, however, a few historical kernels to be gleaned from the Gospels, and these in themselves say quite a lot. We know, for example, that Jesus of Nazareth really did live in Judea apparently during the reign of Tiberius Caesar. And his crucifixion unquestionably belongs to history; a death reserved for the most heinous criminals was not the kind of death a community would have chosen for its hero. Jesus was certainly a Jew, and we know from his recorded words that he was familiar with the beliefs and traditions of the monotheistic Judaism of his day. Few would doubt that he was a man in whom a powerful teaching and unusual healing ministry were at work. Finally, the Church's proclamation of the Resurrection has historical beginnings, as do the persecutions which followed. Except for the above, almost everything else in the New Testament is theological rather than historical in nature.

It is the proclamation of his Resurrection that makes Jesus quite unique among the religious characters of history. Were it not for this belief, there would be no Church and no Bible. "And if Christ has not been raised, our preaching is void of content" (1 Corinthians 15:14). Although Jesus was indeed a great moral teacher, this is not the main reason why he is remembered. The Resurrection is the key, but who can believe such a thing?

After all arguments in favor of the Resurrection have been advanced, belief rests, finally, on the words of those who maintained they experienced the risen Christ — namely the apostles and several others from the inner circle of devotees. No one saw Jesus rise from the dead, and even his missing corpse can be explained away as a theft. But the fact that this belief brought scorn and, eventually, martyrdom to those who first proclaimed it lends weight to their testimony. Even an atheist must admit that, rightly or wrongly, the apostles and their communities really believed that Jesus of Nazareth rose from death to new life.

We, today, even with the help of modern scientific investigation, cannot prove whether Jesus did or did not rise from the dead (the Shroud of Turin notwithstanding). With those who first heard the proclamation, we can either accept or reject the message. Many through the ages have chosen to reject the Gospel on various grounds, the most frequent being that it is a story fabricated by fanatics to assuage their embarrassment caused by following a teacher who was crucified. And look how many unusual stories and religious claims we find among the religions of the world. Certainly, we have neither time nor patience to give our attention to every capricious whim or fantastic tale that confronts us during our few years on earth. Something about the Jesus story is qualitatively different from most cultists' claims and fanatics' promises, however. What if he really *did* rise from the dead? What if it *is* true? Because rejection of this story and its implications would constitute such a devastatingly major life blunder if it is true, serious consideration by everyone must be a minimal response to the Gospel.

The Good News

Many theologians have noted that there is very little in the moral teachings of Jesus that cannot be found already developed in Judaism and even in secular humanistic philosophies. (His teaching on love of enemies seems solely his own, however.) Christianity has no monopoly on ethical wisdom, and history shows us that Christian morality has often borrowed from secular philosophies in its expression (as in the Church's use of Aristotelianism to articulate its natural law morality). If, then, Christianity is not primarily a moral philosophy, what is it?

A reading of the New Testament will reveal that it is the person — not just the teaching — of Jesus which forms the basis of early Christian faith. The Good News has to do with a new spiritual power which the risen Christ brings to all who seek relationship with him and strive to live a life of love. It is never supposed that the ethical imperatives of Christianity can be lived out solely on the basis of unassisted human willpower. God dealt with sin by sending "his Son in the likeness of sinful flesh as a sin offering, thereby condemning sin in the flesh" (Romans 8:3). The Good News has to do with the action of God in our behalf through the person of Jesus of Nazareth.

To understand Paul's short summary of the meaning of Jesus described above we should recall that the New Testament presupposes a world in which the power of sin predominated in the affairs of humanity. The story of Adam and Eve and their proud rebellion against full relationship with God was invoked by Jews as the explanation for the origins of sin in the world. Each generation added its own measure of selfish rebelliousness to the generations before, entrenching society in traditions oppressive to both individual and communal development. By striving to live according to the laws of God revealed through Moses and the prophets, the Jews hoped to minimize the fruits of sin in the world. A Messiah would come one day; and he would redeem Israel from its suffering plight, bringing the nation grandeur and world renown. Such was the hope that sustained the Jewish spirit. Against such a backdrop, we can appreciate the significance of Jesus of Nazareth. His life, teachings, death, and Resurrection came to be seen as decisive in the spiritual evolution of humanity.

First of all, Jesus came to be recognized as the Revealer — the one who answered humankind's primary religious questions. "What kind of a God is God?" Jesus answers: a loving, creative Parent who is unconditionally committed to the well-being of all of humanity, who is with us always, and who feels with us even our most trivial and mundane human experiences. "What does God expect from people?" Again Jesus replies: only that we love God and that we develop and utilize our talents in loving service to our neighbor. This is God's position and invitation through Jesus (see John 15:9-10). God's power is love, and we are left free to accept or reject that love. God will not preempt our freedom by forcing his vision upon us.

But what about evil? Dare we love if, finally, sin has the upper hand? To this, Christianity responds with an emphatic "YES!" Jesus' confrontation with the secular and religious authorities of his day brought about the unleashing of all the powers of sin against him. Institutionalized pride, arrogance, and righteousness were met by him with simple words of truth or else in silence. For this he was rewarded with mockings, scourgings, and crucifixion. In order to preserve the status quo and, supposedly, to prevent the world from slipping further into the drudgery of sin, the authorities decided that Jesus of Nazareth had to be killed (see John 11:49-50). At his death it appeared that Jesus, despite his exemplary life and beautiful teachings, was simply another victim of sin. "Not so," says the Church. By rising from the dead, Jesus showed that God's power is stronger than sin. In Jesus, God suffered the worst of all possible onslaughts from sin and came out victorious. Hope for progress unto goodness and truth has finally been legitimized; the fatalism of the dualists may now be dismissed.

In addition to his roles as Revealer and Redeemer, Jesus is also recognized as the one who sanctifies us in the Spirit. Jesus "first received the promised Holy Spirit from the Father, then poured this Spirit out on us" (Acts 2:33). The cornerstone he laid for life may be built upon by those who cling to him in faith and, consequently, participate in his risen life. ''The Spirit we have received is not the world's spirit but God's Spirit, helping us to recognize the gifts he has given us'' (1 Corinthians 2:12). By building our identity in Jesus Christ and by claiming the power of his Spirit to live our lives in loving service to God we attain our fullest human potential. Life becomes charged with meaning, our inner selves filled with confidence. Even our sufferings can be meaningful when we persevere in this ministry; for the Spirit of God is especially close to us during those times. Christians profess this life to be the best possible way to live our years on earth. And, as if that were not enough, we have, further, a promise of eternal life with God to help sustain our hope.

Toward belief in Jesus Christ

Many self-help programs require, as successful completion of this Step, only that one acknowledge some Higher Power as a Source of health and sanity. This Higher Power need not be Jesus Christ and may not even be a spiritual being. I have known alcoholics who initially considered their AA group as their healing power. Then there are those whose capacity for religious faith is so rudimentary that they designate a tree or a mountain as their Higher Power. Happily, most people move beyond this primitive faith level as time goes on, many even reestablish contact with their previous religious traditions.

In Twelve-Step program context, this second Step helps to solve the problem. It offers hope to one whose first Step has brought insight into powerlessness. Step 2 assures us that our condition can be bettered, but only with help from outside of ourselves. This is the true meaning of our Higher Power.

Unfortunately, it is not eminently clear that just any Higher Power will, indeed, lead us to health and sanity. Life experience teaches us that there will be times when support groups, friends, family members, helping professionals, and even trees let us down when we really need them. If one chooses to designate Higher Power status to some Spiritual Being, then one may ask why it should be believed that this Being cares a microdot about human health or happiness. Nothing in creation and human experience points unambiguously toward a God who loves us unconditionally and desires our utmost happiness. Nothing or no one except Jesus of Nazareth, that is.

If we believe in Jesus as the one who can help us realize our fullest human potential, we need to define what is meant by the word *belief*. Belief can mean many things, but for our purposes here we are encouraging as minimal an intellectual assent to the notion that Jesus of Nazareth is a model of the God-charged life. This assent need not be completely free from doubt (it never will be). But we should be able to say with Saint Peter and company: "Lord, to whom shall we go? You have the words of eternal life. We have come to believe; we are convinced that you are God's holy one" (John 6:68-69).

In Step 1 we saw that selfishness is anti-growth; now we need only recognize Jesus as the one who can lead us out of that smug death into spiritual health, vitality, and meaning. It is probably obvious by now that this basic level of faith will have to be affirmed in life again and again. In truth, we are never completely finished with any of the Twelve Steps. We can make real progress in the depth of our growth, however.

Personal Reflection

1. If you have not done so lately, read the New Testament, especially the Gospels. When you come to sections you do not understand, make a list of questions for discussion with another Christian, a priest, or a minister. Try to get a feel for

the overall statement about Jesus proclaimed in the Gospels. Once you get a perspective on Jesus, you might then venture into other New Testament writings.

2. Find a Christian community that manifests the fruits of the Holy Spirit: "love, joy, peace, patient endurance, kindness, generosity, faith, mildness and chastity" (Galatians 5:22-23). Experience their worship and find out what they believe and why. Communities, like individuals, will never be perfect; but try to avoid extensive involvements in groups that seldom talk about Jesus or that are rigid, self-righteous, and unreasonable.

3. Make an appointment to talk about Jesus with a priest, minister, or mature Christian who is knowledgeable of the Scriptures. Share your doubts with them, but be open to their words.

4. Find books about Jesus or Scripture that address your spiritual needs. Ask your Christian friends for recommendations if you do not know where to begin.

5. Hear Jesus asking, "Who do you say that I am?" (Mark 8:29) What is your response?

Group Discussion

1. Let each member of the group answer Jesus' question: "Who do you say that I am?"

2. Why is the Resurrection such an important Christian belief? What do you believe about the Resurrection?

3. How did Jesus reveal God to us?

4. What do Christians believe about Christ's redemption?

3

We decide to turn our lives over to Jesus Christ

To many people this is a terrifying Step, conjuring up thoughts of religious fanaticism and otherworldly saintliness — attitudes entirely foreign to their mentality. It is one thing to consider the possibility that Jesus of Nazareth revealed God and that he rose from the dead, but quite another to become involved in his story. Some fear that getting serious about Jesus will mean that they will be obliged to jaunt off into the jungles of South America to convert bare-skinned natives, while fighting off mosquitoes and snakes; others have visions of being called into a life-style that will be rigid, moralistic, and generally dull. These and other resistances to conversion are understandable, for the invitation to change one's life-style can evoke fears. But most resistances are based upon misconceptions of what it means to be a Christian.

Being a Christian means following Jesus Christ. It means rooting one's identity in the person of the risen Christ and acting according to his will. In short, being a Christian means living a life of charity, recognizing Jesus to be the incarnation of charity itself; it means thinking and acting as Jesus does but in the uniqueness of one's own individuality. Living this kind of life is not easy, for the struggle to be charitable brings us constantly in conflict with our selfish desiring. Working through this struggle is what the Cross is all about.

Human motives and strivings

Every time we make a decision we employ to a certain extent our value system. People do not just do things aimlessly and with no motives, although it might seem that way to an observer from another world. There is a motive for almost all behavior, even though it may spring from the deepest levels of the unconscious. Here are some of the most common human motives and the beliefs which support them:

1. *Pleasure:* The gratification of sensual needs is rewarded in the brain by secretions of certain chemicals which are interpreted as pleasurable. Presumably, sense-gratifying behavior is of survival value, else it would not be so affirmed by pleasure. The abuse of our sensuality through neglect or overindulgence in any area of life results in diminished pleasure in the long run. Materialistic philosophies tend to view pleasure as the ultimate criterion for making personal decisions.
2. *Esteem:* Our need to be regarded favorably by others seems almost inexhaustible. How sweet it is to be given genuine appreciation! The desire for esteem rises out of our human need to be loved and recognized as unique and irreplaceable. In its most perverted form, esteem-seeking behavior becomes a hunger for power, which in turn is rooted in the belief that the strongest are worthiest of love and respect.
3. *Security:* As conscious beings we know that the world is sometimes a dangerous place and that misfortune and death are harsh realities that can intrude upon anyone at any time. We know, too, that we can do certain things to minimize the likelihood that misfortune, sickness, or death will overtake us prematurely. Prudence, discipline, and careful planning,

therefore, have their place as important virtues, for we cannot grow into mature human beings if we are too insecure. But people who have an extreme distrust in the unpredictability and unmanageability of reality become paranoid about security; they begin to act out their fears in ways that are often eccentric and destructive.

We could certainly identify other motives for behavior in addition to pleasure, esteem, and security, but we treat only these three because they form the basis for the most important schools of psychology established in this century. No one will have trouble recognizing any of them in his or her daily movements of will; one or mixtures of the three probably explain most of what we have decided to do during much of our lives. Each has its proper place in our human strivings; all can become destructive if overemphasized.

Christianity recognizes the validity of our desires for pleasure, esteem, and security and advances a set of propositions about reality which promise to enhance our experiences of each.

1. *Pleasure:* Because Christianity does not espouse a materialistic view of the universe, there is little danger that Christian beliefs can be used to fan the embers of an unhealthy desire for pleasure. More than pleasure, Christianity promises joy, a state of spiritual well-being only hinted at in our experiences of pleasurable sense-gratification (see John 15:9-11).
2. *Esteem:* God, the Creator and Sustainer of the universe, regards each person as precious. To make this experience real, the Holy Spirit moves us to form communities of people committed to affirming the dignity and importance of each individual.

3. *Security:* Even though we all experience accidents and will eventually face death, Christians take heart in their belief in an afterlife. Because Jesus rose from the dead, we, too, shall rise to new life. We are immortal spiritual beings, and our heavenly Father's will is ultimately sovereign in the universe. God, our Father, is a providential God, forever leading us into contact with people and circumstances that are grace or help to us in our time of need.

Far from depriving us of the best of human experiences, Christianity enhances them by affirming beliefs which, if we embrace them, allow us to live life to the full.

The realization of Christian dimensions of pleasure, esteem, and security is contingent on a faithful following of Jesus Christ. A new life principle or motive for behavior must be pursued — one which transcends pleasure, esteem, and security while recognizing their validity. That life principle is *love* or charity. By charity, here, we do not mean the kind of gift-giving usually associated with a condescending kind of pity but a new force which empowers us to love even our enemies. "Love is of God," wrote Saint John, and "everyone who loves is begotten of God and has knowledge of God." Furthermore, "God's love was revealed in our midst in this way: he sent his only Son to the world that we might have life through him" (1 John 4:7-9). If we want to know what love looks like and how love behaves, we need only look to Jesus.

The Christian life principle

Before discussing the meaning of living a life of love, we should come to a better understanding of love in general. It is unfortunate that this word has come to mean so many things in the English language — everything from loving one's child to making love to loving a particular television show. The Greek language distinguishes between different kinds of love, and, in his book *The Four Loves,* C. S. Lewis describes them as follows: *storge,* or affection, is the kind of love parents feel for children and vice versa, and also the fondness we might come to feel for certain people, pets, and even material goods by virtue of familiarity; *philia,* or friendship, bonds people together under the umbrella of common interests; *eros,* or romantic love, entwines lives in the interest of sexual fulfillment and the perpetuation of the species; *agape,* or love, is gift-love or love that comes to us through no merit of our own and with no ulterior motives. *Storge* helps us to meet our security needs; *philia* brings us some measure of esteem; *eros* is the goddess of pleasure. Without *agape,* however, any of these loves can become so predominant as to make of us slaves to their movements. *Agape* enables us to experience all of our human loves more intensely while keeping them in perspective. ''In such a case the Divine Love does not *substitute* itself for the natural — as if we had to throw away our silver to make room for the gold,'' concluded Lewis. ''The natural loves are summoned to become modes of Charity while also remaining the natural loves they were.''

Becoming a new person does not mean abandoning our human loves for the sake of God's love — unless, of course, these human loves lead us to wrongdoing. Becoming a Christian means beginning, within the context of our present lives, to utilize the Christian life principle in all our undertakings. We must begin to ask ourselves not what will bring us pleasure, esteem, or security, but what is the loving thing to do. By thus striving to conform our lives to the shape of love, we will realize our deepest experiences of pleasure, esteem, and security.

Because Jesus of Nazareth is the incarnation of love itself, our struggles to live a life of love can be aided immensely if we look to him for guidance and support. "What would Jesus do?" is the question we must ask ourselves. And the answer will be a clear statement of the Christian life principle. We must begin to make decisions as Jesus himself might make them, and this will require from us a growing knowledge of who he is. The best of formal knowledge concerning the life of Jesus will have to be studied in order to help us keep an objective perspective on our journey; a passionate devotion to Christ will enable the Spirit to reveal his will in our minds and hearts. Prayer, Scripture, Church teaching, and community will become essential and indispensable means for informing and empowering us to live in love. Our lives will thus become a lived-out relationship with the risen Christ rather than a mere commitment to Christian ethics. In time, our decision-making processes will almost automatically respond "as Jesus would." When we reach that point — and few seem to attain this level of development in this world — we can be sure that our attitude corresponds to Christ's (see Philippians 2:5).

Just how far should we go with this love or "What would Jesus do?" decision-making principle? Is it to be employed in making decisions of even the simplest and most mundane kind? If I am trying to decide whether to use my fifteen-minute break to speak with a friend at the office or to have a cup of coffee and read the paper alone, should I ask myself, "What would Jesus do?" Jesus said: "If you can trust a man in little things, you can also trust him in greater" (Luke 16:10). Our most significant battles in life are won and lost according to how we deal with the little things that come our way day after day. Large problems seldom just happen; they are usually an accumulation of small problems now come to a head. Similarly, great lovers have grown in virtue by deciding to love in little ways through each and every day. The Christian life principle must be employed whenever we are conscious of making decisions, and that includes even the most trivial.

Does such a close and determined effort to follow Jesus mean that we shall lose our individuality? Not at all! We may find a few changes occurring in personality, but that is a more superficial level of personhood anyway. Our personalities are those aspects of ourselves that we choose to show to the world. Hopefully, personality will become more conformed with individuality, which is the deeper self standing ever before God. Only those who sacrifice even their individuality and judgment to cult leaders and other perverters of the Word of God become truly lost. God, on the other hand, always leaves us free to accept or reject grace, and therein lies our deepest level of freedom. Proud refusals to obey God's will do not make a person more individual — only more self-righteous and, hence, more unhappy. Using individual judgment to choose God's way enables us to become more free and more unique. This is a great paradox, but a wonderful reality to be embraced.

Following Jesus is a great adventure that will move us into new and unpredictable experiences. There are few absolutes to guide us along the way, but the following guidelines can help us to understand some of the parameters of love:

1. Recognizing all people (including ourselves) to be unique and important children of God and, therefore, treating them accordingly — with acceptance and respect.
2. Developing our talents to the full and utilizing them in ways that promote health of body, mind, and spirit in ourselves and others.
3. Extending to others the opportunity to develop their gifts and

express them appropriately in an environment free from oppression.

4. Being honest and truthful in all areas of life.
5. Forgiving those who have wronged us and apologizing and making amends to those whom we have wronged.
6. Striving to change social structures and/or traditions that inhibit the realization of the above.
7. Relying upon God for guidance and strength in living out this life.

All of this and more will the following of Jesus Christ demand from us. It's a large order, to be sure, but it's the only challenge that seems worthy of the totality of our human nature. Besides, Jesus never said it was going to be easy.

Faith and the Cross

"The message of the cross is complete absurdity to those who are headed for ruin, but to us who are experiencing salvation it is the power of God" (1 Corinthians 1:18). "We adore thee, O Christ, and we bless thee, because by thy holy cross thou hast redeemed the world" is a beautiful Catholic prayer. What is the significance of the Cross? Why do Christians find it so important?

If we are to answer the above questions, we must remember that the Cross was the world's reward to Christ for living a life of pure love. Love led him into confrontation with all of the forces of evil institutionalized in his day, and he responded by placing his trust in the goodness and justice of the Father while embracing the instrument of his own death. Only by doing so was he able to break the power of sin in the world; had he run from the Cross, God's power to save could not have been so conclusively revealed.

When we attempt to follow Jesus by living a life of love we can expect to come face-to-face with the power of sin every day. Our desires to realize pleasure, esteem, and security in selfish ways will confront us at every turn, and we should expect this. Those who find it necessary to take a stand concerning political and social issues can expect ridicule and persecution. "If you find that the world hates you, know it has hated me before you" (John 15:18). "They will harry you as they harried me" (John 15:20). But by persevering in our attempts to live in love during times of struggle with our own selfishness or during persecutions, we embrace our own crosses and thus help to bring about the transformation of sin into love. Carrying these daily crosses will also deepen our own spiritual identity, for we do not truly become changed within until we displace selfish thinking with love. It is impossible to live this way without faith, of course, but it is also impossible to grow in faith without living a life of love.

What is faith? "Faith is the confident assurance concerning what we hope for, and conviction about things we do not see" (Hebrews 11:1). What is this something that Christians want? We want the world to become God's kingdom (see Matthew 6:10), a place where people can develop, work, and play in freedom, justice, and peace. Even though such a world does not yet exist, we believe that it shall eventually come to pass because Christ has promised us that he will one day return, ushering in an age when his lovers will inherit eternal life (see Matthew 25:31-46). Because we believe that Jesus has risen from the dead, we also believe that it is within his power to make good his promises. People of faith, therefore, learn what God has promised, and build their lives on the premise that God can and will do what he has promised.

Consider some of the incredible promises made by God which apply not only to life after death but also to our present existence:

1. Those who give to the poor shall be rewarded (see Matthew 6:4).
2. God hears our prayers and knows our needs (see Matthew 6:5-9).
3. Those who ask, search, and knock on the doors of life for grace will receive it (see Matthew 7:7-11).
4. God will give the Holy Spirit to those who ask (see Luke 11:9-13).
5. Living according to Christ's way will bring stability into life (see Matthew 7:27).
6. Those who follow Christ shall find rest for their souls (see Matthew 18:19-20).
7. Christ will be present when two or more gather in his name (see Matthew 18:19-20).
8. Christians shall receive repayment many times over in this life for leaving the past behind and following Jesus (see Luke 18:28-30).
9. Those who believe in Jesus shall do the same works that he did (see John 14:12).
10. Jesus will give to his followers a peace that surpasses understanding (see John 14:27).
11. If we remain in Christ, we may ask what we will and we shall get it (see John 15:7).
12. Living the Christian life will bring us joy (see John 16:24).

The list could go on and on! These are all promises that can be tested, and, in fact, have been confirmed millions of times during the course of Christian history. They apply for the most part to spiritual matters, but is this not the area of life where we need the most encouragement anyway?

Making a start

More than any other Step, this one will require from us a lifetime of practice. Step 3 is, for all practical purposes, a summation of all the Twelve Steps. Steps 1 and 2 only establish a rationale for following Jesus; Steps 4-12 outline certain practices which will enable us to live a life of love.

Because Step 3 can never really be fully accomplished, successful completion of it, in this program, requires from us only that we make a start. Conversion is an ongoing process, and we shall never be through with making decisions to turn our lives over to Jesus Christ. But conversion will never happen at all if we simply leave our life direction up to blind chance or capricious mood. A start toward Step 3 should, therefore, include at least the following:

1. A *desire* to build our life in conformity with God's will;
2. *Prayer* for faith in God's promises;
3. Becoming more conscious of motives and beginning to make *decisions to act in love;*
4. *Involvement* in Christian community for learning, worship, support, and service;
5. *Perseverance* in love, even during times of struggle, by praying and by practicing the Serenity Prayer: "God grant me the serenity to accept the things I cannot change, courage to change the things I can, and the wisdom to know the difference."

If we begin to do the above, our lives will change; and we will begin to experience the confirmation of God's promises in all areas of life. Adventure, meaning, peace, and joy will come to us in measures never before experienced. The world's standards of pleasure, esteem, and security will be recognized for what they are: shallow and destructive. Our eyes will be opened, and our hearts will burn with a new vitality (see Luke 24:31-32).

We should keep a journal of our impressions and experiences as we make this fresh start. In the months ahead we will be able to note our progress by reading over earlier entries. In years to come we will treasure these times as precious indeed!

Group Discussion

1. What are some of the ways in which the world invites people to pleasure, esteem, and security?
2. What does Christianity say about pleasure, esteem, and security?
3. Why is it important to have a life principle? How realistic is it to expect people to embrace the Christian life principle of love?
4. What is faith?
5. Have individual members of the group discuss how they face the crosses they experience in daily life.

4

We make a searching and fearless moral inventory

Few of us really enjoy taking a good, hard look at ourselves. Extremely self-righteous people may not mind doing so because they are not as conscious of their defects of character and grossly overestimate their positive assets. Depressives, on the other hand, are not as conscious of their goodness, sinking instead into a quagmire of regrets and pity. But the majority of us fit somewhere between these two extremes, exaggerating some of our strengths and weaknesses while remaining unconscious of major assets and liabilities. If we are to become Christian lovers, this cannot go on.

Step 4 gives us the opportunity to learn how to love ourselves. Remember the Lord's commandment: "You shall love your neighbor as yourself" (Matthew 22:39). If we desire to become more conscious agents of God's incredible love, we must first love ourselves. Only then will we believe that the gifts and talents we share with others are valuable and worth their having. But in order to love ourselves we must first know ourselves, and that is what Step 4 invites us to do. By taking an honest look at ourselves, we will come to know that the love we found in Steps 2 and 3 applies to us as well as to others. God's own forgiving love will empower us to love ourselves and then go out to others in love.

But how do we look at ourselves? If it is true that many of our strengths and weaknesses are buried deep in the subconscious, how can we expect conscious reflection to discover them? In Step 5, we will see that another person will have to become involved in our own journey through this renewal process. Other people can often detect things which elude our own critical self-reflection, and their feedback will reveal some of the blind spots in our character. For the present, however, asking the Holy Spirit to help us become conscious of buried aspects of character is an excellent way to become aware of blind spots. At any rate, we know that certain aspects of our lives will escape our notice this first time around. And this is why Step 10 reminds us that this kind of inventory should be ongoing. For now, however, we are interested in making a decisive new start.

Morality and consciousness

Because this Step invites a moral inventory, we need to understand just exactly what is the true meaning of morality. Most people think of morality as involving the standards for evaluating the rightness and wrongness of behavior. This definition is certainly true, but it is important that we come to grips with the reasons for the rightness and wrongness of certain behaviors. Some people do not ever become conscious of the vision of life implied by their standards of behavior; others accept standards of morality handed on by parents, religions, and secular institutions, but do not struggle to comprehend the wisdom of these ways. Step 4 invites us to become more morally conscious and, hence, more active in living a moral life.

But what is morally good anyway? Who is to say what's right and what's wrong? Hitler believed that he was doing good by destroying the Jews; Truman believed that by dropping two atomic bombs on Japanese cities he was doing a good thing (or the lesser of many bad things); some believe that sex before marriage is permissible; others believe that even after marriage sex ought to be shared in gentleness and respect. By what standards do we evaluate the morality of human behavior? Isn't morality a subjective and relative matter?

Christianity does not accept the notion that goodness is whatever anyone says it is. For Christians, morality means acting in love or doing what Jesus would do. There are many areas in life where our moral choices do not come to us in neat black-white dualisms; but even in moral grayness our focus is still defined by the clear call of Christ to treat each other in a loving manner. There is no room here for acting out of social convention or peer pressure unless the standards in question also happen to fall in line with the law of love.

For Christians, love is not the *ends* we seek as a consequence of our actions; love is a *means* to bringing about its own realization. Hitler may have rationalized his slaughter of the Jews by envisioning a utopia where the living would be happy; but a Christian can never justify using sinful means to try to produce a desirable end. The lessons of history on this point are quite clear; sinful means do not produce sinless ends because ends are always the products of means. The Crusades and the Inquisition were well-intentioned movements designed to achieve noble and admirable ends; but they were marked by injustices and other wrongful means, leaving their ends unrealized and the historical record of Christianity tarnished in a most embarrassing way. In undertaking our Step 4 inventory, we will look not only at our intentions but especially at the results of our behavior.

It is important that we understand, too, that Step 4 invites us to become more consciously aware of ourselves. By consciousness, here, we mean becoming more aware of our motives, feelings, thoughts, and options in the present moment of existence. Conscious awareness makes it possible for us to realize what our choices are in a given situation and, hence, to pursue a response that we might not have considered if we were not consciously seeking it. This is what Jesus meant when he spoke about laying down his own life (see John 10:17-18) and not letting other people take it from him. Conscious people are proactive; unconscious people are merely reactive, behaving as instinct, conditioning, and the whim of the moment dictate. Unconscious people unwittingly serve the power of sin in the world because they usually get caught up in the world's pursuit of pleasure, esteem, and security. They are gullible and easily manipulated. Conscious people are more capable of choosing the good, even when everyone around them is choosing evil, because they are more likely to recognize alternatives that unconscious people never even dreamed of. So we can say that as Christians we should strive to become more consciously loving and lovable.

If the words *goodness* and *love* still seem too abstract and nebulous to you, read again the section from Step 3 entitled "The Christian life principle." Unless you are aware of the Christ mirror, into which you must gaze in order to evaluate the morality of your actions, Step 4 will be difficult for you. Do make a start on it, however. Perhaps after beginning you will become more conscious of the morality of your actions.

Personal Reflection

(The questions which follow are intended to stimulate the kind of moral awareness invited in Step 4. Answer each one honestly. Take as long — days, weeks, months — as is necessary for you to come to grips with these issues. Write your reflections in a journal so that you will be able to remember them when you undertake completion of Step 5. Before each reflection period, take a few minutes of quiet time, calling on the Holy Spirit to help you to love yourself and become more aware of yourself.)

Self-awareness

1. What are three of your most unique talents? How are you using them?
2. What do you think you do best? How often do you do this?
3. What do other people like most about you? How often do they show you appreciation for your gifts?
4. Are you a hopeful person? Why? (Why not?)
5. Are you a happy person? Why? (Why not?)
6. What do you regret most about your life? Why? How have you handled this regret?
7. What do you perceive to be your greatest weakness? When and how does this manifest itself in your life?
8. Are you a patient person? When is impatience a problem for you? How do you express impatience?
9. What do you do for play or fun? How often do you allow yourself the opportunity to have fun?
10. How important to you are friends? Do you believe you are valued by others as a friend?
11. What does your family mean to you? With whom are you closest? Most distant? Why?
12. Are you a patriotic person? Why? (Why not?)
13. How do you feel about your body? Do you neglect your health? What are you doing to take care of your health?
14. How do you feel about your sexual identity?
15. Is it easy for you to relate with members of the opposite sex? Why? (Why not?)

16. Do you try to develop your mind? Why? (Why not?)
17. What do you believe about God?

Moral Awareness

(For each of the questions below, consider your relationships with family members, relatives, friends, working acquaintances, casual relationships, and even people in other cultures and communities. In your journal, jot down a few notes concerning these relationships so that you will be able to call them to mind when you meet your confidant(e) for Step 5 completion.)

1. Do I recognize other people to be unique and important children of God, accepting them and treating them with respect?
2. How am I developing my talents and utilizing them to serve others?
3. Am I truthful and honest in my dealings with other people?
4. What specific wrongs do I need to forgive in people I relate with on a regular basis?
5. Have I been faithful in keeping my commitments to others?
6. Do I strive to resist evil and to help those who are oppressed?

Group Discussion

1. Read your answers to the questions in the "Self-awareness" section. If you feel comfortable, share them with others.
2. What criteria do you use in evaluating the morality of your behavior?
3. Do you agree with the statement "Sinful means cannot produce sinless ends"? Why? (Why not?)
4. How does a person grow in conscious awareness?
5. Does consciousness guarantee moral goodness? Is it possible for a person to be consciously immoral?

5

We admit to God, to ourselves, and to another human being the exact nature of our wrongs

More than anything else, we need unconditional love. Without it, food, clothing, and career opportunities are lacking, our self-worth low, and energy spent. What we all need is to know that we are lovable and capable even when we fail or when other people reject us. Only unconditional love nurtures this kind of wellness in us.

Jesus revealed the amazing fact that God — the ultimate reality of the universe — loves each individual person unconditionally all the time. He made this known through his teachings and, especially, through his actions among us. Where he found sickness he extended healing; when he was persecuted he forgave; when people stagnating in selfish life-styles encountered him he challenged them forth unto growth. Everywhere and at all times he let it be known that the welfare of the individual human being mattered more to him than anything else in the world. Jesus gave us a clear and unambiguous message: "God loves you!" Saint Paul later pointed out that nothing — not even persecution and death — can separate us from God's love (see Romans 8:31-39).

Most of us lack this awareness of being loved personally and unconditionally by God. Perhaps it is because our parents loved us conditionally, or perhaps we have experienced unfortunate events in life which lead us to doubt the insanely generous nature of reality. With all the injustices, accidents, earthquakes, floods, etc. in the world, many people reject the fact that God loves individual human beings. There are times when accidents happen and ill fortune befalls us; but we know that God loves us nevertheless. ''Whoever is dear to me I reprove and chastise'' (Revelation 3:19).

Many people misunderstand the Christian teaching concerning the sovereignty (controlling influence) of God. They assume that all events in this world — even accidents and injustices — occur because God wills it so. But the ministry of Jesus belies this notion of sovereignty, revealing that many things happen which God merely allows to take place. What God wants for us is love, growth, peace, health, and prosperity in an environment of justice, freedom, and opportunity. God's dominion over the world demands that these values eventually leaven society; but, because of humankind's freedom of choice, they will not come without turbulence and suffering. What is unfortunate about a mistaken notion of God's sovereignty is that it leads people to blame God for the misfortunes that happen to them at a time in life when they most desperately need to open themselves to the healing compassion of Christ. Our God is with us in bad times as well as good; he always loves us unconditionally.

Unburdening

Those of us who have spent our lives trying to earn love by achieving goals or by impressing others will not find it hard to believe that God accepts us in our strength. What is difficult for all of us, however, is believing that we are lovable even when we are weak and/or sinful. Many times we shut off these areas of life from consciousness because they are too unpleasant to behold and thus threaten the fragile self-concept to which we so desperately cling. Such denial and defensiveness are counter-productive, allowing destructive energies to influence us more than we would like. The only way out of this diabolical maze of low self-concept, defensiveness, and trying to earn love is belief that God and other people love us even in our weakness.

Step 4 helped us to get in touch with our strengths and weaknesses and so attain a measure of self-knowledge that is a necessary prerequisite to genuine self-love. Now it is time to turn this awareness into acceptance.

Step 5 is the way to self-love, turning old self-perceptions into self-acceptance. Many people in Twelve-Step programs have likened Step 5 to scraping barnacles from the hull of a ship. It is true that our psychospiritual ships are still floating in the sea of life, but how much more freely will they sail if freed from the excess emotional baggage we lug around because of low self-worth? This will be a painful process for most of us, but the freedom and love which will be ours for doing so are certainly worth the price.

We begin by moving into prayer, calling upon the risen Christ to be with us as we prepare to read over our reflections from Step 4. It might be helpful to read the parable of the Prodigal Son (Luke 15:11-32) to remind us of God's loving forgiveness. Next we share with God our understanding of our strengths and weaknesses, speaking out loud in honesty and sincerity as though he were sitting in a chair listening to us. If we feel moved to cry, we allow ourselves to do so; repentant weeping can be a powerful cleansing experience. We should take as much time as we need and not rush the process. When we feel (believe) that we have expressed everything that laid heavy on our heart, we should reread the parable of the Prodigal Son, noting the response of the father to his two sons and rejoicing in God's unconditional love for us.

Confession

Most people appreciate the value of self-revelation before God, but cringe at the thought of doing so before another human being. God is spiritual, after all, but other people are so *real!* The reality of other people forms the basis for the wisdom of Step 5, however. It takes considerable humility to bare our souls before God; baring our souls before others is the ultimate in ego-deflation, and that is precisely what we need in order to reverse our selfish defenses.

Christians who maintain that it is not necessary to confess our sins and weaknesses to one another simply do not understand the importance of the Incarnation. God intended that his work of love and forgiveness be spoken among us and not remain transfixed in a book of Scriptures. That's why Jesus came: to make the Word flesh. He even gave his apostles and their successors the power to forgive or retain sins (John 20:23), insuring that his work of reconciliation would continue forever. This does not nullify the redemption that Christ won for us by his crucifixion; it does indicate the truth that God's grace works through our relationships with one another.

Christianity is an incarnational religion. We believe that God became human to show us in concrete ways what love really means. God did not express his feelings toward us by thundering from the sky or through other feats of majesty. He became a man and spoke to us in ways that we could understand. Jesus revealed a human God and invited us to become godly humans. This means that we must now extend to each other the same kind of love that God extended to us in Jesus. We, too, must incarnate God's spirit in our lives, making his love as real for each other as Christ did among us. This is the basic meaning of the Incarnation.

Completion of Step 5 requires that you (the reader) admit to another human being the exact nature of your wrongs. This confidant(e) should be a person who will listen patiently, who will accept you without judging you, and who will help you at times to understand what you are trying to articulate. This person will be God's ears to you; his or her words of acceptance will communicate God's unconditional love for you. You may decide to choose a priest, a minister, a family member, or even a complete stranger to hear you out. The choice is up to you.

If your confidant(e) is not familiar with Step 5, you might want to brief him or her on what kind of session you seek. (You might let your confidant(e) read this chapter.) It is important that you make it clear that you are not seeking counseling or advice. Such a person is there to listen and to help you express yourself. After the session is over, you might never see this person again and that is fine; you might, on the other hand, want to continue the relationship, perhaps in a counseling or spiritual direction setting, and that is also up to you.

Complete self-disclosure to one individual is quite different from the partial disclosures we share with certain friends in our lives. Partial disclosures allow us to be selective and manipulative, keeping intact our defenses while giving us the illusion of humility. After going through the Step 5 experience, many individuals find it possible to share themselves more deeply with others. With our self-worth more deeply rooted in awareness of God's unconditional love for us, there is no need to try to earn the love of others by impressing them. Real honesty will become a norm in everyday living for a person who completes this Step. The clarity of thought and peace of mind produced by such authentic living is well worth the risk of self-disclosure.

Group Discussion

1. What does it mean to love someone unconditionally? Is it possible to do this and still disagree with a person?
2. How do you reconcile the notion of God's love for individuals with the fact of injustice, sickness, and accidents?
3. What is your response to the objection, ''God forgives my sins, so I don't need to tell them to anyone else.''
4. How do we continue the Incarnation in our own lives?

6

We declare ourselves ready to have God remove all our defects of character

People in Twelve-Step programs usually find Steps 1-5 so rewarding that they want to stop there, ignoring the other Steps or else regarding them as only marginally relevant. This kind of attitude will surely undermine spiritual growth, however. Those who have worked all Twelve Steps and have a wider perspective of the program claim that Steps 1-5 help us only to make a start in the right direction. The only interpersonal risk called for has been in sharing with the Step 5 confidant(e), who, at any rate, is counseled beforehand to be exceptionally gentle and accepting. Attitudinal and life-style changes in the direction of love have been encouraged all along, but now is the time to really get at the crux of our problems. In Step 6 we declare ourselves ready to begin making changes in our character.

One assumption underlying Step 6 is that we must sincerely desire to change destructive aspects of our character before lasting improvements begin to take place. That is why this Step is devoted to provoking an attitude of readiness. Most people recognize the destructiveness of sin in their lives, but how easy it is to excuse those self-destructive practices, and how difficult it is to let go of them completely! ''What we must recognize now is that we exult in some of our defects; we really love them,'' so we are advised by AA. This kind of attachment to character defects opens up for us the wide road to perdition that Jesus warned us about (see Matthew 7:13-14). If we are to experience the peace and joy that come from pursuing the narrow road to spiritual growth, we must surely let go of our perverse attachments.

Are you ready?

Common defects of character

Christian tradition has long recognized the insidious ways in which sin produces and then promotes certain defects of character. In the early Church, pride and lust were regarded as sure pitfalls to spiritual growth. Other sins were later added to the list, and we have the modern listing of pride, avarice, lust, anger, gluttony, envy, and sloth, all of which are called the "seven deadly sins." (More accurately, they are vices which lead to other sins.) Contemporary ministers have often avoided utilizing traditional concepts concerning sin, grace, and virtue, but the wisdom of the ages has much to tell us about human nature and God's workings in our nature. Here we will review some of the subtle ways in which the seven deadly sins lead us away from growth.

The questions below are intended to help you as you prepare to change your destructive character defects. You might want to use your journal to jot down notes for each question.

1. *Pride*
    (a) Are you willing to let go of your desire to impress others? In what areas of your life will this be most difficult?
    (b) How difficult will it be for you to avoid conversations

which slander others? When does abuse of this sort usually take place in your life?

(c) Is it easy for you to "give credit where credit is due" when discussing your accomplishments with others?

(d) How would your conversation be affected if you were to purge it from self-serving exaggerations and white lies?

(e) Do you ever find yourself trying to chart your life so that you do not need others? How important is self-sufficiency to you?

2. *Avarice*

(a) Do you ever horde material goods under the pretense of legitimate prudence ("just a little nest egg for the future")? What is the difference between fiscal prudence and greed?

(b) For the sake of money, have you ever compromised your values? Is it easy for you to refuse this temptation?

(c) Suppose you were offered a better-paying position whose acceptance would require you to do work which you loathe. Would you accept or refuse?

(d) Can you decide what an adequate amount of money for your needs might be and then content yourself with that much only?

3. *Lust*

(a) Do you encourage lustful thoughts under the guise of "appreciating beauty" or "healthy sex-drive"? Are you ready to discourage this kind of voluntary fantasizing on your part?

(b) How willing are you to avoid movies and reading materials which utilize explicit sexuality for the sole purpose of arousing you sexually?

(c) Do you indulge in "innocent" flirtations in pretense of "just having a little fun"?

nonfattening (and even noncarcinogenic). Letting go of defects of character does not consign us to the realm of the dullard.

Are you ready to become more conscious of and responsible for the development of your character? If you have reflected upon the questions concerning the seven deadly sins and found that you are rather sick of the phoney games they require you to play, are you ready to move along? When you can respond affirmatively to these questions, you will be ready to go on to Step 7.

Group Discussion

1. What are some of the ways in which our culture invites us to succumb to the temptations of the seven deadly sins?
2. Can you think of examples from the Gospels that show Jesus struggling with temptations? How did he resist them?
3. How important for your spiritual growth is the attitude of readiness described in this chapter?
4. Share with the group some character defect that you have been struggling to change and have made progress in disciplining. Tell them what helped and what did not help you to change.
5. Share with the group your responses to the questions concerning the seven deadly sins. (Feel free to avoid those questions you find uncomfortable to discuss.)

7

We humbly ask God to remove all our shortcomings

Christianity maintains that God is actively involved in the shaping of creation and the lives of human beings. God is considered to be far more than a philosophical concept or an ethical necessity; God is a living Person, whose love for us empowers us to rise above our lower selfish nature so that we might live in peace and harmony with ourselves and others. In order that we might realize this vision of the kingdom of God on earth, we are given grace, or help, without which we would be left entirely to ourselves and our own resources. Faith puts us in touch with God's grace and enables us to consciously experience spiritual power in our lives.

Jesus revealed God's hope that we might love one another. "I give you a new commandment," he said. "Love one another. Such as my love has been for you, so must your love be for each other" (John 13:34). His life plumbed the depths of God's incredible love, and it serves today as a model for our own lives. So important was it to Jesus that we comprehend the significance of God's call to love that he devoted his ministry of teaching, healing, and prophecy entirely to this truth. He influenced people to turn away from sin, encouraging them to gouge out their eyes or cut off their hands if these parts of the body caused them to fall (see Matthew 5:27-30). Although such cautions may be deliberately overstated, they do point up Jesus' desire for us to change destructive ways of behaving.

Those of us who have struggled on our own to try to change compulsive behaviors can deeply appreciate our need for grace. In Step 6 we examined our attitude toward self-destructive compulsions, traditionally known as the seven deadly sins. If we are indeed ready to move away from these pitfalls to growth, we are now in a position to ask for and receive the graces from God needed to make changes in our lives.

God will give grace to anyone attempting to change his or her behavior in conformity with the ways of love. When we ask for this kind of help from God, we may be sure that we are asking "in his name" and that he will affirm and respond to our desires (see John 14:13-15). This kind of petitioning is quite different from praying for good weather or for a raise in pay. God may or may not grant such requests; God will always come to our assistance when we struggle to love, however.

Many people in Alcoholics Anonymous adorn their cars with bumper stickers which read, "I believe in miracles; I am one." We should all be so conscious of the ways in which grace has transformed us from children of the dark into children of the light. Any change in character which leads us away from selfishness toward love is a sign of grace working in our lives. Anyone or anything which helps us to do this is grace to us.

Channels of grace

At first glance it might seem that this Step 7 emphasizes only a private, pietistic approach to change. This is not so. The truth is that God gives grace through other people and creation as well as through prayer and worship. For example, it is a mistake to assume that God heals only through faith healers and not through doctors and counselors. Even if they are atheists, doctors and counselors who enable us to return to health become grace to us.

If we are serious about having God remove all our shortcomings, we ought to consider utilizing the agents of his grace whom he has gifted and placed at our service. Failure on our part to do so might indicate that we have, perhaps, not really finished with Step 6 or that we are not so ready to be humble before God in seeking help as Step 7 requires. A person who is a compulsive worrier would do well to see a counselor as well as pray for the grace to accept things as they are; likewise, overindulgers in food and/or alcohol need professional help. Priests, ministers, parents, and friends can help us to grow in many ways; the fragile simplicity of nature can remind us of our own inherent poverty of spirit; spiritual writings are grace to our understanding; the whole world can communicate grace to the spiritually conscious person. We should, therefore, pray that God will release us from the shackles of our character defects and that we will have the courage to seek help when we need it.

Virtue

It is important that we understand the meaning of virtue because Step 7 presumes that we are practicing it. The way we remove our shortcomings is through the practice of virtue. Through the centuries, theologians have distinguished between supernatural (theological) virtues and natural (cardinal) virtues. Faith, hope, and charity are called theological virtues because they refer to God: we believe in him, we trust in him, we love him. They are gifts from God. We believe in God because God has revealed himself to us; we hope because we believe that God's will is sovereign; we love because he loved us first. The initiative lies with God, although we are encouraged to pray for faith, hope, and charity. We might experience growth in these virtues by putting them to use in our lives; but we can take no credit for their presence, for they are gifts that we do not earn.

Cardinal virtues are practices and disciplines which we can initiate with our free will to help us become better channels of God's grace. They enhance the realization of the theological virtues, which in turn empower us to grow in the cardinal and other natural virtues. Prudence, justice, fortitude, and temperance are called cardinal (from the Latin *cardo:* hinge) because upon them many other natural virtues depend.

Once we understand their meanings, it will be easier to practice them in our lives.

1. *Prudence (wisdom)* directs the intellect to judge as good only those things suitable for attaining our ultimate end, God. It presupposes knowledge of the world and of the Scriptures, both of which require considerable study. We use this acquired wisdom to make judgments in private life and public affairs — all in the service of love.

2. *Justice* means giving to others what is rightly theirs and avoiding interference in what is another's. Respect for human rights and equitable treatment to all form the cornerstone of justice, without which societies grow turbulent and oppressive. Justice is required not only between person and person but also between persons and the community and between the leaders of the community and the community itself. Obviously, too, the virtue of religion (rendering to God due worship) is a matter of justice.

3. *Fortitude (courage)* requires that we become assertive enough to risk for love's sake. We must become involved in the world and be willing to become vulnerable at times if we are to practice fortitude. Patience and perseverance are

obviously related to this virtue. Playing it safe in life is the antithesis of this virtue.

4. *Temperance* — in today's world — usually connotes abstinence from alcohol, but as a cardinal virtue it emphasizes disciplines that lead to self-control, especially of bodily passions. Moderation might be a better word for this virtue, which helps us experience inner freedom. Meekness, forgiveness, and humility also flow from its use. Simplicity in life-style is temperance practiced to the fullest degree.

Both theological and cardinal virtues are effective antidotes to the seven deadly sins. They give us a profile of the kind of person we are to become and inspire us to leave behind our character defects, replacing them with strengths that will lead to peace and joy.

Personal Reflection

1. Look over your reflections from Steps 1, 4, and 6. Identify the defect of character that has been most troublesome to your spiritual growth. Ask God to give you the grace to change this behavior. After a few days, begin working with another defect of character.
2. Pray for the grace to grow in faith, hope, and charity.
3. Make a list of ways in which you can be more courageous for the advancement of truth and love. During the next week, make a conscious attempt to practice at least two of these suggestions each day.
4. In what areas of your life do you most need to practice moderation? Share your struggles about this problem with someone, and ask him or her to help you develop a plan and hold you accountable for making progress toward moderation in this area.

5. Begin the practice of reading spiritual writings which can help you to grow in wisdom. Commit yourself to reading at least one book or booklet a month. You might want to join a discussion group where you can talk about a book with others.
6. Do not refuse to join the fight to help others who are poor and oppressed. Find ways in which you can contribute your time, talent, and money to help advance justice in the world.

Group Reflection

1. Share your reflections on any of the above suggestions.
2. How does grace break into your life? Share with the members of your group your understanding of grace.
3. How can the cardinal virtues help you to resist the seven deadly sins?
4. "Personal growth is growth in grace and virtue." Do you agree with this statement? Why? (Why not?)

8

We make a list of all persons we have harmed, and determine to make amends to them

Christianity is a religion emphasizing deep, loving relationships among people. In John's Gospel, we hear Jesus praying that all believers will be one in him and with one another. "I living in them, you living in me — that their unity may be complete. So shall the world know that you sent me, and that you loved them as you loved me" (John 17:23). Luke tells us that early Christian communities lived out Christ's prayer for unity in a revealing and inspiring manner. "The community of believers were of one heart and one mind. None of them ever claimed anything as his own; rather, everything was held in common" (Acts 4:32). Although the early Church suffered persecution from Roman authorities, many people were attracted to the community life modeled by these Christians. "See how they love one another," they noted in obvious admiration of the people they so little understood. Would that the same could be said of us today!

Unfortunately, the early Christian utopia did not last. Right from the beginning, certain people within the community sought to hold back on their giving for selfish reasons (see Acts 5:1-11). Later, too, the community's teachers seemed to have lost their common understanding of the meaning of Jesus' life, death, and Resurrection, splitting the Church into factions (see 1 Corinthians 1:10-13). And today the numerous divisions in the Body of Christ constitute the greatest scandal to Christianity, providing many nonbelievers with a sufficient rationale to justify their lack of faith.

Many of the present-day rifts in the Church come from a misunderstanding of what is essential and what is not. The essential truth about Baptism, for example, is that the ceremony be performed with water and in the name of the Father, Son, and Holy Spirit. Whether a person is immersed in water or has water poured on him or her is not the essential point.

Now it is an essential truth of Christianity that Jesus came to redeem us. ''He died for all so that those who live might live no longer for themselves, but for him who for their sakes died and was raised up'' (2 Corinthians 5:15). And Saint Paul continues by saying that God ''has reconciled us to himself through Christ and has given us the ministry of reconciliation'' (5:18). Jesus himself taught us that reconciliation with God also means reconciliation with other human beings (see Matthew 6:12, 18:23-35). This, too, is an essential truth of Christianity, and it is what Step 8 encourages us to realize.

Steps 1-7 have helped us to get our own house in order, but that is not all there is to becoming a new person. We must also get our relationships in order! Ongoing personal growth will not be possible if we do not break free from the shame and guilt we carry because of wrongs we have done to others. Like barnacles on a ship's hull, our past wrongdoings prevent us from sailing as smoothly as we should, trapping us instead in rationalizations that only bring mental fragmentation and divisions in our families and communities. Clearing the air with others is a Step which we must take for the sake of our relationships and for our ongoing reconciliation with God as well.

Reconciliation

"To err is human; to forgive divine" is an old saying. The contrasts in that proverb might become even more clear if we were to state the human condition completely: "To err is human; to seek revenge is also human." Forgiveness does not come easily or naturally for us; retribution seems to be the more common human response to wrongdoing in cultures throughout the earth. "An eye for an eye and a tooth for a tooth!" is a form of justice sought not only by the ancients but by modern secular societies as well.

Our attempts at exacting justice from one another often spawn more wrongdoing than is corrected. Cycles of violence, for example, are fueled by accusations from both sides that wrong was done them at some time in the past and so should be avenged. Cycles of hatred and hard feelings in our families and communities are similar in that we look to each other's wrongdoing in order to justify our vindictive behaviors. Seldom is it possible to discover from whence began the injustices and transgressions we so righteously oppose. The Bible tells us that it all began with Adam and Eve's rebellious independence, inferring that these attitudes go back to our earliest human origins.

Into our world of vengeance, violence, and whirlwinds of righteous anger stepped Jesus, telling us to turn the other cheek, to love our enemies, and to pray for our persecutors (see Matthew 5:38-48). Only then, he implies, will cycles of violence be broken. If we do not seek revenge against those who wrong us, the fires of hatred in the world are deprived of fuel for their destructive furnaces. Justice will be meted out by God in the end, at which time those who spent their lives provoking offense will receive their just deserts (see Matthew 13:36-43).

Many people interpret Jesus' nonviolent response to evil as somehow condoning evil. Nothing could be further from the truth! Saint Paul reminds us to resist evil wherever we find it by doing good (see Romans 12:21). And Jesus himself confronted the evils done by the religious leaders of his day with daring words and actions which ultimately cost him his life. But he approved of no vengeance that would harm others (see Luke 9:54; Matthew 26:51-53), insisting that unjust means could never produce just ends (see Matthew 7:16-20, 12:33-37).

Christians are to be agents — "ambassadors," Paul calls them — for reconciliation. This means that we, in our lives, must break the cycles of broken relationships that surround us by doing good and opposing evil, by offering forgiveness and seeking forgiveness. We must *initiate* reconciliation in our broken world, even venturing out to meet with people who, rightly or wrongly, hold something against us (see Matthew 5:23). If our gestures are refused, then there is not much that we can do about that; we cannot control the response of others. But we must try; any failure to do so only guarantees more brokenness and violence in an already fragmented world.

Making a list

As we begin to take seriously our charge to become reconcilers, we will need to examine our relationships at home, in our communities, and even those in the world at large. If people have harmed us in any way that has provoked a lasting hardness of heart toward them, we must learn to forgive. We may or may not choose to let them know this verbally, but we ought to demonstrate our forgiveness by acting toward them in ways which indicate that we hold no hard feelings toward them. This will not always be easy, but the grace to forgive will be ours if we ask for it.

But there is more — and this is the hard part for most of us! We all have harmed other people in various ways through the years. In Step 9 we will need to seek out these people and make amends with them if doing so will serve the truth in love. For now, we need only identify who those people are, how we have wronged them, and how our lack of forgiveness has affected us and them mentally, emotionally, financially, and even physically. We begin with our immediate circle of family and friends, then reflect on those relationships at work and even the most casual of friendships. Remember, we are only making a list here; in Step 9 we will discern what should be done about it.

Because this will be a list which we alone should see, we should take great care that the wrong person will not come upon it and learn our secrets. If our right to privacy in our own home is fully respected, our diary or personal journal might be the best place to write our reflections on this Step. We should take as much time as we need and do a thorough job. Honesty with ourselves in these matters will be a cleansing experience.

Here is a simple way to make out the list:

Person/Relationship	My Wrongdoing	Effect on Others	Effect on Me
1. Susan Jones, Wife	1. Angry outburst about housecleaning.	1. Anger, coldness, resentment.	1. Guilt, shame, loss of self-respect.
2. Deborah Q., Secretary	2. Made sexual advances toward her at company party and on other occasions.	2. Distrust of me; does not cooperate with me at work.	2. Loss of self-respect; she doesn't help me; fear that she will tell Susan.
3. Smith Enterprises, Employer	3. Falsified expense account; padded it.	3. Company's loss about $75.00 but does not know it.	3. Guilt; fear that I shall be discovered.

Group Discussion

1. How responsible are you for difficulties people are having in countries where your tax dollars support repressive regimes?
2. Why is it important to clear the air of past wrongdoing if we are to grow spiritually?
3. Discuss some of the ways in which the "eye for an eye" mentality shows up in our culture?
4. Do you find it more difficult to forgive or to seek forgiveness?
5. Share an example of forgiveness from your life or from the life of another that inspires you.

9

We make direct amends to those we have harmed, except when to do so would injure them

There is little disagreement among Twelve-Step program members that this is both the most difficult and most cleansing Step of all. It would have been difficult to start with this one because we might not have even thought that making amends would be necessary. Also, there was the problem of our own low self-worth and lack of discipline. But now, after experiencing God's love, finding acceptance by our Step 5 confidant(e), and then committing ourselves to the avoidance of sin while growing in virtue and grace, we are in a position to take this most courageous Step. It is time to balance the scales of justice in our lives as best we can, seeking forgiveness from those whom we have harmed and making restitution if necessary.

The most common objection to Step 9 is that it is simply unnecessary. "Each one of us has harmed other people at some time in the past," some people will say. And others: "Why not let bygones be bygones?" It may well be that some of our wrongs can be forgotten and laid to rest; but far too many still stand as barriers between ourselves and others. There are those whom we have hurt and then later ignored because relating with them again brought to mind our own weaknesses. Then there are those situations where we have done wrong and "gotten away with it" but now live with fear that we shall eventually be discovered. How many of us shudder when we read in the paper that a person has been caught at a crime he or she committed years ago?

Step 9 provides us the opportunity to become active in getting our lives in order. Clearing the air with those we have harmed will bring tremendous relief to us and will undoubtedly surprise and inspire those from whom we seek reconciliation. Like a balloon anchored to the earth, we have been held down by our guilt thus far. Now is the time to begin untying those enslaving attachments to our past so that we can become more fully committed to living and loving in the present. Now is the time to begin to fly!

Making restitution

In order to complete this Step, you will need to look back over your Step 8 list to determine the proper course of action you should take regarding the incidents you listed. You will wonder whether or not you should simply let an incident be, saying nothing about it while committing yourself to more respectable behavior with the person in question; maybe you will realize that you need to apologize to someone, but don't know when or how this ought to be done. These are difficult situations, and a confessor or a spiritual director can help you discern your responses to each. The following considerations should be helpful in this regard.

How much does this person (or company or institution) know about some negative behavior of yours — for example, wasting time on the job? If they know nothing and are not aware of having been hurt in any way by you, perhaps you can let bygones be bygones; however, you should now begin to proceed in a more positive manner. But what if you have stolen money or cheated in some other manner? Justice requires that you repay what you have stolen! Coming forward and admitting guilt might cost you your job, or — in the case of nonpayment of income taxes — you will be subject to a legal sanction of some kind. In such cases you will have to weigh these risks against everything else. Fortunately, the Federal government provides a means — with no questions asked — for conscience-stricken citizens who are guilty of tax evasion. And the same can be done in reference to cheating or stealing in other areas — through anonymous donations to the institution or persons concerned. A simple rule for dishonesty and theft is this: Repay what you owe. If you do not do this, you will retain your guilt, and self-righteous rationalizations will further contribute to selfishness and character defects.

What if you have done something wrong and another person has been blamed for it? And what about the incidents like an extramarital affair when one of the spouses is completely unsuspecting of the infidelity in question? What about relationships that are dishonest but not tragically so — like flirtations or romantic crushes, for example? Perhaps no one but yourself is aware of the indignity of your behavior in some of these cases, but what does Step 9 require that you do about them?

Ask yourself two questions to help you determine whether apologies or amends are in order: *Will an apology help me to grow in relationship with this person?* and *Will my apology help the person and/or others in question more than it will hurt them?* If you can answer an unequivocal "Yes" to both questions, then you need to begin planning your reconciliatory approach; if you answer "No" to both, then let the matter die. If you are not sure about either, then talk it out with someone until you are sure. Perhaps a couple of examples will serve to illustrate how this process might work out.

Suppose you have been involved in an extramarital affair about which your spouse knows nothing, but many of your co-workers suspect what is going on and a couple of them know for sure. You decide to terminate the relationship and commit yourself anew to your marriage, and your lover understands this and reluctantly sets you free. Need you tell your spouse all about this? Probably not! But what about those co-workers and their gossipy tongues? What if they let on to your spouse? You should tell them that the affair is now over and that you are trying to make your marriage work out; and then ask them to promise that they will keep your secret and give their support in your commitment to your spouse. If your spouse finds out about this in the future, then you can admit the truth and explain how you tried to patch things up without causing excessive turmoil. People are more likely to forgive your infidelity later on — after it is all over — than if you had gone straight to your spouse early on, seeking forgiveness.

What if, in the above example, your lover tells your spouse about the relationship because he or she is not impressed with your Step 8 dedication? You will have to tell the truth, of course, and hope for the best.

As for those sex-related flirtations that no one — not even the "flirtee" — is aware of, let them be! There is no point in rocking a boat when no one even suspects waves. "While we may be quite willing to reveal the very worst, we must be sure to remember that we cannot buy our own peace of mind at the expense of others." This is excellent advice coming from AA. If the relationship poses an ongoing problem and source of temptation for you, you will have to discuss it with the person in question, perhaps making logistical adjustments to minimize the danger.

As the above examples illustrate, there are circumstances which do not call for apologies. Be careful in discerning these, however. There is a difference between prudent silence and evasion; in the former, the good of the other is at stake, in the latter, only selfishness. Except for the kinds of circumstances described in the above examples, Step 9 calls for an initiative on your part to apologize to those whom you have harmed and to make amends if necessary.

Set up a schedule, listing whom you will speak to, what you will say, and when you will say it. Writing letters and making phone calls are very acceptable ways to communicate your sentiments to others; face-to-face meetings are often impossible to arrange and may not be the best approach for some people at any rate. The important point is that you must initiate reconciliation now — before it's too late! You won't live forever, and neither will those you have harmed. You will feel much better about yourself and your relationships with others after you have made all possible amends.

Group Discussion

1. Do you believe that it is sometimes better to leave things unsaid, or must you always be completely truthful with others?
2. How important is it that you alter your life-style to minimize the negative effects you have on the people in your family? On people in other cultures and countries?
3. How do you feel when a person who has wronged you seeks your forgiveness?

10

We continue to take personal inventory, and promptly admit when we are wrong

If we have made serious efforts to complete Steps 1 through 9, we have undoubtedly begun to experience levels of peace and joy hitherto unknown to us. "Can we keep it up?" many people wonder at this point. "Or is this all some kind of flash in the dark — a nice growth experience, but only a passing fad?"

Step 10 comes at a critical point in our renewal process, affirming the progress we have made thus far while pointing the way toward continuing spiritual growth. Our troubles in the past were a result of our own unconsciousness and lack of reflection. We allowed little problems to build up day after day until they became big problems. Our lack of conscious commitment to growth in grace and virtue allowed character defects to become malignant, rendering us far more vulnerable to the power of sin than would have been the case had we practiced discipline. If we are to continue to build on the good foundation we have laid, we shall have to practice Step 10 on a regular basis.

To begin, then: What do we mean by personal inventory? Must we forever go through long, drawn-out reflections such as those undertaken in Steps 1, 4, 6, and 8? Isn't it unhealthy to overanalyze ourselves? These are some of the questions that come to mind at this time.

By personal inventory, we mean regular, ongoing examination of our strengths and weaknesses, motives and behaviors. Saint Ignatius of Loyola considered this to be as important as daily prayer because he, like many other spiritual masters, discovered that it is very easy to regress in the spiritual life. "If you're not progressing, you're regressing," so say the spiritual giants of the ages, all of whom practiced Step 10 in some manner during their lives. Regular inventory need not be a monumental affair, however. It might take up little more than fifteen minutes per day — a small price to pay for continuing the good work we have begun.

Types of personal inventory

Examining motives and behaviors can be done in a number of ways, each of which has its own advantages and limitations. Some of the most common means of taking inventory are discussed below.

1. *Spot-check:* This means stopping for a few moments several times a day to review what has been going on with you. What have you been feeling? Have you been acting out of love or selfishness? If you have wronged anyone, now is the time to admit it and to make amends.
2. *Daily Consciousness Examen:* It is good to stop at the end of each day to look over what has gone on and how you were involved. This examen time generally lasts about fifteen minutes, so you will have to set aside time to do it.
   (a) Settling in: Spend a few moments getting comfortable. Relax. Try to clear your mind of distracting thoughts, but do not be disconcerted if you do not succeed at this completely.

(b) Prayer: Thank God for your day and for the graces you have been given. Ask the Holy Spirit to help you look back on your day and see your behaviors and motives as God saw them.

(c) Examen: List some of the key events of the day in your journal. What were you feeling during those times? What kinds of thought patterns formed the basis of your feelings? Were you acting in love or selfishness? Jot down a few notes in response to these questions.

(d) Resolution: Identify the character defect or circumstance that is the most significant cause of your difficulty. How will you be struggling with this problem in the future? In terms of love, what might you be able to do to work through this difficulty? Write out a short plan of action and read it over tomorrow morning.

3. *Days of Recollection and Retreats:* These are special days, weekends, or even weeks when people devote themselves fully to hearing the Word of God addressing the word of our lives. There are a variety of options available, including silent, preached, and group experiences.

4. *Spiritual Direction:* Meeting regularly with a mature Christian to share how your life in Christ is coming along usually involves some time spent in taking inventory. The spiritual director is one who is committed to holding you accountable for your own spiritual growth; he or she will usually want to know what's happening in your life, so inventory time is usually a normal part of the session.

5. *Support Groups:* Meeting regularly with a small group of Christians committed to supporting each other as they live their lives in Christ is another resource for your ongoing growth. Many of these groups encourage you to share your inventory during the meeting so that group members can

help you to work through issues you are facing at the moment. Group members can often provide helpful feedback concerning the way you relate with others.

After reading the above, you probably realize that you cannot utilize all these resources every day. A minimal Step 10 commitment ought to include spot-checks three or more times a day, daily consciousness examen, and an annual day of recollection or retreat. Many people enjoy biweekly support group meetings and monthly dialogues with a spiritual director in addition to their daily routine. Such a program will not turn you into an overanalytical ''navel-gazer,'' nor will it involve an unreasonable commitment of time from you. If growth in love is your number one priority in life, you can scarcely afford to neglect this discipline.

People who take inventory regularly become more conscious of their assets and liabilities. They are less likely to yield to their feelings of anger and loneliness in self-indulgent ways because they are more emotionally balanced. The aimless drifting through life that characterizes so many people does not apply to them; they know who they are, what they want, and where they're going. They are therefore more capable of becoming conscious lovers, which is the goal of Christian life.

Group Discussion

1. ''If you're not progressing, you're regressing.'' Do you agree with this statement? Why? (Why not?)
2. How does ongoing self-examination help a person to grow spiritually?
3. Share some of the ways you are practicing this Step in your life.

11

We seek through prayer and meditation to improve our conscious contact with God, praying only for knowledge of his will for us and the power to carry it out

Jesus was the greatest psychologist who ever lived. Long before Freud, he understood that human behavior is ultimately rooted in our vision of ourselves and reality. "A good man produces good from his store of goodness; an evil man produces evil from his evil store," he tells us, adding: "I assure you, on judgment day people will be held accountable for every unguarded word they speak" (Matthew 12:35-36). Aligning our behavior in conformity with love will require that we come to think the way Jesus thinks — to see the world the way God sees it. Spiritual reading and study can contribute to this process, but prayer and meditation are indispensable.

If we are to become new persons, we must not only put to death old ways of thinking but also put on a new mind. "Do not conform yourselves to this age but be transformed by the renewal of your mind," wrote Saint Paul in Romans 12:2. Spot-checks and consciousness examen inventories can help us identify what is going on in our minds; prayer and meditation reshape our minds according to the mind of Christ.

Most people recognize the value of prayer, but too few people practice it faithfully. "I don't need to take prayer time because my life itself is a prayer" goes one popular excuse. "People don't need to pray; all that's important is that we do good" goes another. However, many of the spiritual geniuses saw things in a completely different way. They did not value prayer because it helped them to do good works, but saw prayer as the more valuable end which good works helped to deepen. They valued prayer as the most important discipline in their lives; they prayed daily.

Private prayer

"Prayer is lifting up the mind and heart to God," states an ancient definition. The evangelists often call attention to the many times when Jesus took time alone to lift his mind and heart to the Father. If Jesus, the begotten Son of God, found such a need for prayer in his life, how much more do we need to pray?

There are many books and pamphlets suggesting different ways to pray. We will have to discover the style that is right for us as individuals, of course. But it is doubtful that we will ever experience the benefits of prayer if we seek it with the wrong attitude.

Many people approach prayer as though they hope, through their prayer, to arouse a sleeping and indifferent God. Spiritually mature people maintain that it is the other way around: We pray because a loving God, who is eager to communicate with us, wants to arouse us out of our spiritual sleep and indifference. Prayer is God's idea. The attitude we should bring to prayer is one of being present to a God who is already present to us. Only then will the following suggestions on how to pray make any sense.

1. *Solitude:* "Whenever you pray, go to your room, close your door, and pray to your Father in private," commanded Jesus in Matthew 6:6. There is indeed much to be said for communal prayer, but private prayer cannot be replaced by any other activity. We must go some place where we can be alone and undisturbed; being alone with God is what is meant by solitude in prayer.

2. *Silence:* "In your prayers do not rattle on like the pagans. They think they will win a hearing by the sheer multiplication of words" (Matthew 6:7). Prayer time should be quiet time. Any words and sentiments exchanged with God are done in the context of silence.

3. *Time:* Jesus spent entire nights in prayer; few of us can last fifteen minutes. Any time spent in prayer is probably better than no time at all, but it is doubtful that inner silence and a receptive listening to God's Word can take root in less than twenty minutes. Prayer time should also be prime time. Do not wait until you are tired and sleepy, for example, because it will be difficult to lift your mind and heart to God.

4. *Eliminating distractions:* Most people come to prayer with their minds filled with all sorts of thoughts and feelings, much of which is little more than mental static. Telling God what you're thinking and feeling is one way to clear your mind; deep breathing and repeating a calming word such as "Jesus" or "Abba" is another way to clear up the static. Still, distractions are not easy to eliminate, no matter what approach is used. Few people succeed at this discipline completely, so you should not be discouraged if a bit of distraction lingers all through prayer time. Be patient with yourself here; simply call your mind back to God whenever it strays. Saint Francis de Sales believed that this in itself is a valuable practice.

5. *Listening:* You pray because you have something to say to God and he has something to say to you. But if you do all the talking, you shall never hear his word. After quieting your mind somewhat, read a short passage from Scripture and take it as being written just for you. Use your imagination to re-create the scene if possible.

6. *Reflecting/meditating:* After reading a passage from Scripture (or from a spiritual book), ask yourself: What is this passage saying to me about God? about my life? These and other questions should be pondered during meditation time. Keep at this process until you have exhausted the passage of its meaning (for the time being, at least). Then jot down a few notes in your journal for later examination.

7. *Acts of thanksgiving, petition, and sorrow:* This movement may be more natural for you early on during your prayer period. The timing is not really all that important. Thanking God for gifts bestowed and asking help in time of need come naturally to everyone, but it is less easy to make acts of sorrow. So tell God here that you are sorry for the many times you have failed to love him properly. You should also pray for yourself and others and for peace on earth. In the words of Saint Alphonsus: "Prayer can do everything. What we cannot do by our own strength, we can do easily with the help of God obtained through prayer."

8. *Acts of adoration:* If you feel moved to spend time praising and adoring God, be thankful for this very great grace. Loving God with your whole heart, mind, and soul is an experience you can sometimes enjoy during prayer. Be open to this contemplative grace, for prayer of worship is not just for mystics only. God wants everyone to pray in this manner. These acts of adoration plant God's seeds of love deep within the heart; and those seeds will produce a hundredfold

(see Mark 4:20) because they have fallen on fertile soil. Saint Augustine claimed that prayer of adoration was the greatest joy a human being could experience. You must not leave the face of this earth until you know what he was talking about.

If you set aside a regular time to practice the essentials of prayer discussed so briefly above, you will surely become more consciously aware of God's presence in your life. You will walk about in this turbulent world with a quiet place in your heart to conquer the temptations and absorb the emotional shocks that come your way each day. Your emotional life will become more stabilized; you will experience inner freedom as never before. God's will for you will become more apparent, and the power to live out an obedient response will be given you.

Communal prayer

Many of the foregoing elements of private prayer can be experienced in communal worship. Most services center around the hearing of God's Word; there is a minister who leads the reflection on the Word; time is allotted for petitions and prayers of thanksgiving; often too, there is time given for adoring God in silence. Both private and communal prayer are necessary for spiritual nourishment.

When you pray together in community you recognize the value of your shared life in Christ. God, after all, is Trinity, and the most important goal of love is community. A Christian without a community is like a fish out of the water: Such a one drowns. In community you experience a small taste of what God's kingdom is like: You leave the world behind for a little while to make love more real for yourself and others. Your prayer in community is, therefore, very important, helping you to become more consciously aware of God's will for you as Step 11 encourages.

Communal prayer takes many forms. Most Protestant services feature singing and preaching; Pentecostal worship is affective and spontaneous; the Catholic Mass combines the Liturgy of the Word with the Liturgy of the Eucharist to celebrate the Bread of Life given and received in a daily community ceremony. In truth, all of the Catholic sacraments are prayerful celebrations of the community — each signifying a special presence of Christ with his people. In each case, communal prayer is combined with private prayer. Both enrich and deepen us in unique ways.

Group Reflection

1. How do you pray? What benefits do you experience from prayer?
2. What are some of the ways that you have found helpful in eliminating distractions during your private prayer?
3. How does communal prayer affect your private prayer and vice versa?
4. When can a person truthfully say, "My life is a prayer"?

12

Spiritually awakened as a result of these Steps, we are determined to carry this message to others, and to practice these principles in all areas of life

Some Christian writers have summarized the movements of personal growth as three: "Accept yourself, be yourself, and share yourself." This is what we have been doing in this program — with an emphasis on the fact that our true "self" is not our selfish, craving ego. Our real identity, we have discovered, is in Jesus Christ. "Your life is hidden now with Christ in God" (Colossians 3:3). And by "hidden" Paul does not mean that we make no mention of Jesus in our lives; he is simply calling attention to the fact that our lives are now mysteriously caught up in Jesus' own story.

Step 12 affirms all the progress we have made thus far and encourages us to share the Good News of Christ with others. We do this because we have already had a spiritual awakening and, therefore, must, by now, appreciate the graces we have recently received in our lives. If we are honest with ourselves, we will realize that many of these graces have come to us from God through other people. These persons at some time in the past influenced us in ways — perhaps ever so small — that eventually made us seriously consider the real meaning of being Christian. It is now our turn to do the same for others.

But how do we carry the message to others? And how can we be certain that we have had a spiritual awakening in the first place? Most of us will probably feel better about ourselves as a result of persevering through the first eleven Steps. Is that what is meant by a spiritual awakening? Finally, there is the question of practicing these principles in all areas of life. Which principles? We have learned many things during this time, and it will be hard to remember them all.

This final Step can be divided into three separate but related topics: spiritual awakening, evangelization, and daily living. We will examine each in some detail in order to respond to the above questions.

Spiritual awakening

One of the most overused words in our society is the word "spiritual." In this book we have suggested what it means to be a spiritual person, and we have undertaken practices to help us to become more spiritual. We have seen the vast difference between the spiritual life and a life governed by selfishness.

Being a spiritual person means being aware of God's presence and seeking to do his will in our lives. This kind of awareness and commitment is different from a mere awareness of one's personal goals, values, and feelings. A spiritual person does have goals, values, and feelings, but these are embraced by a deep love for God and a burning desire to please him. Persons who are only psychologically motivated might well be committed to Christian values; but without the kind of faith that comes from spiritual motivation they will not experience the wonder of being loved in the core of their being. Spirituality is, therefore, inextricably bound up in faith, without which it is difficult to know and please God.

"What then is the point in being spiritual if we can be good without a conscious faith commitment?" some might ask. This is a good question, because it recognizes the fact that spiritual people do not have a monopoly on ethical behavior. Being a spiritual person will probably guarantee ethical behavior from us more consistently than if we were simply striving on our own to do good. As spiritual beings, we recognize all people to be children of God, and so we cannot in peace turn our backs on injustices of any kind. We are committed to nurturing our identities as ambassadors for reconciling the world in Christ. It is Christ's own desire and vision that moves us to do good. Caring humanists have no such perspective to help keep their attention and energies so focused on love.

Commitment to the spiritual life does more than move us to loving behavior. Cultivating and nurturing Christian spirituality will enable us to experience life here on earth to the full (see John 10:10). We will come to know depths of life and feel ourselves responding to life in ways that others cannot fully understand (see 1 Corinthians 2:10:16).

By recognizing the fact that you have already had a spiritual awakening, Step 12 affirms the likelihood that you are, by now, somewhat aware of God's presence in your life and that you have begun to build your character in Christ. Ongoing work with Steps 10 and 11 will be especially helpful in deepening your spiritual awareness. Even so, you will never feel as though you have fully arrived in spiritual consciousness here on earth. Always will it seem as though you are "seeing a dim reflection in a mirror" (see Corinthians 13:12); you are only beginning to awaken spiritually.

Evangelization

People in most cultures are raised to mind their own business. So when others try to tell them what they ought to believe about this life and the afterlife, they generally lend them a deaf ear (or else tell them where to get off). Few of us like to be preached at; we don't like to be pushed into doing anything that makes us feel uncomfortable. Yet, this Step tells us that we are to "carry this message to others" — to some, of course, who don't even want to hear it.

Step 12 does not advocate being pushy or preachy. There are ways to communicate the Good News in a receivable manner, and we will examine a few shortly. But first we must be sure that it is, indeed, a message of *Good News* that we have to share. If our life in Christ does not produce peace and joy in our character, then why should an already-miserable humanity pay us any heed? Who has not been preached at by some dour, righteous soul who looked as though the burden of the whole world was upon him or her? And how far did this get with us? Therefore, we must not even attempt this part of Step 12 until *we* are good news; if we attempt evangelization prematurely, we will only be hurting ourselves and others.

The most effective form of outreach is not planned but comes naturally during the course of everyday life. If people who rub shoulders with us begin to recognize a special "something" that we have, they might eventually ask about it. This is the ideal situation, for the fact of their inquiring means that they are probably ready to listen.

Each day, too, usually brings many opportunities to communicate our values. All groups at some time discuss local or world events, practicing armchair philosophy and politics with gusto. When this happens — and we may even choose to raise an issue occasionally — we should share our beliefs humbly and simply, avoiding condescending insinuations that we are right and others are wrong. We Christians are often completely wrong in our perceptions and understanding of world events, and so we should never assume that our faith in Christ guarantees us infallible wisdom.

Sharing with others our own approaches and experiences in working through life's problems is another way to make the Good News receivable. People are far more interested in applied philosophy than in theoretical conjecturing. Ministers have found on many occasions that their congregations perk up when they not only talk about an issue but share how they struggle with it in their own lives. Telling someone how we pray, for example, is usually more interesting to them than a discourse about why everyone should pray, what prayer is, etc. If we can talk about our own experiences in living a spiritual life, other people will be more inclined to listen to us.

Finally, we evangelize by reaching out to those in need. There is a story about a Hindu man who lay dying as Mother Teresa sought to comfort him. "What is this?" the man asked, grasping the crucifix that hung from her neck. "That is a symbol to remind me of my God," she replied. "Your God is now my God!" the Hindu exclaimed with his last ounce of strength. Charity in action speaks louder than words.

Daily living

Life often seems so mundane and our involvements so lacking in any potential for meaning that the phrase in Step 12, "practice these principles in all areas of life," can seem totally irrelevant. As we become more spiritually awakened, however, we will probably become more aware of many opportunities to act lovingly. Perhaps we will even grow out of our present job into another one that allows us to utilize our potential more fully on a regular basis.

As we have noted many times already, love is the virtue that we are called to practice in our daily lives. Love is our focus and Jesus is our living Guide. The struggle to live a life of love will remind us of the seven deadly sins we must avoid and of the virtues we must cultivate. It is true that there is a lot to remember in living a life of love, but that is because life itself is filled with many rich and sometimes complex experiences. We do not struggle with our own unaided willpower alone, and that is part of the Good News. Jesus promised to give us a helper — the Spirit of Truth — to lead us to the complete truth (see John 16:13).

If we regularly clear our minds of mental static, then we will become more sensitive to the gentle whisperings of the Holy Spirit in our own minds. If we practice these Twelve Steps in our lives — especially Steps 10 and 11 — we will fill our minds with thoughts and memories which the Spirit can use to remind us of God's way when we need to hear it. Practicing these Twelve-Step principles in our daily affairs is a real possibility when we have such a Guide to show us the way.

All Twelve Steps demand ongoing practice. You never finish conquering your selfishness, so you must constantly retake Step 1; your need for God (Steps 2 and 3) will only grow through the years; self-analysis, reconciliation, and growth in virtue (Steps 4-9) are always needed; inventory (Step 10) and prayer (Step 11) prevent you from backsliding into egocentricity. Discipline, practice, grace, and time will eventually work together to mold loving instincts in you if you persevere in working these Steps. The hardest part is to begin, but you have already done that.

Group Discussion

1. How do you feel toward people who are pushy in trying to get you to believe as they believe?
2. In what ways did other people influence your own faith development?
3. If a person can be good without being a Christian, then why become a Christian?
4. Share some of the ways in which you evangelize in your everyday life.
5. How do you experience spiritual awakening in your life?

The Twelve Steps
of Alcoholics Anonymous

1. We admitted we were powerless over alcohol — that our lives had become unmanageable.
2. Came to believe that a Power greater than ourselves could restore us to sanity.
3. Made a decision to turn our will and our lives over to the care of God as we understood Him.
4. Made a searching and fearless moral inventory of ourselves.
5. Admitted to God, to ourselves, and to another human being the exact nature of our wrongs.
6. Were entirely ready to have God remove all these defects of character.
7. Humbly asked Him to remove our shortcomings.
8. Made a list of all persons we had harmed, and became willing to make amends to them all.
9. Made direct amends to such people wherever possible, except when to do so would injure them or others.
10. Continued to take personal inventory and when we were wrong promptly admitted it.
11. Sought through prayer and meditation to improve our conscious contact with God as we understood Him praying only for knowledge of His will for us and the power to carry that out.
12. Having had a spiritual awakening as a result of these steps, we tried to carry this message to alcoholics, and to practice these principles in all our affairs.

The Twelve Steps reprinted for adaptation with permission of Alcoholics Anonymous World Services, Inc.